MEDIEVAL ARCHITECTURE

THE GREAT AGES OF WORLD ARCHITECTURE

GREEK *Robert L. Scranton*
ROMAN *Frank E. Brown*
EARLY CHRISTIAN AND BYZANTINE *William L. MacDonald*
MEDIEVAL *Howard Saalman*
GOTHIC *Robert Branner*
RENAISSANCE *Bates Lowry*
BAROQUE AND ROCOCO *Henry A. Millon*
MODERN *Vincent Scully, Jr.*
WESTERN ISLAMIC *John D. Hoag*
PRE-COLUMBIAN *Donald Robertson*
CHINESE AND INDIAN *Nelson I. Wu*
JAPANESE *William Alex*

MEDIEVAL ARCHITECTURE

European Architecture 600-1200

by Howard Saalman

GEORGE BRAZILLER · NEW YORK · 1962

All Rights Reserved
For information address the publisher,
George Braziller, Inc.
Number One Park Avenue
New York 16, New York

International Standard Book Number 0-8076-0336-8

Library of Congress Catalog Card Number: 62-7530

Seventh Printing, 1983

Printed in the United States of America

CONTENTS

This brief essay is an introduction to some major buildings and problems of medieval architecture. The author has based his discussion on a survey of the older and more recent literature in this vast field and on his own observations abroad. The ideas presented reflect—without presuming to reflect upon— the lessons learned at the feet of three distinguished scholars: Guido Schoenberger, Richard Krautheimer, and the late Ernst Gall.

8

H. S.

Carnegie Institute of Technology
Pittsburgh, Pennsylvania

The continuing evolution in our understanding of the political, religious, and artistic centers of gravity of Late Antiquity has had a decisive effect on current approaches to the problems of medieval architecture. The various roles played by Rome, Constantinople, Antioch, Jerusalem, Milan, Ravenna, Naples, Trier, the coasts and hinterlands of Yugoslavia, Greece, Asia Minor, and North Africa as well as Spain, the Alps, France, the British Isles, and the Rhine Valley from the third to the seventh centuries have been gradually clarified by the persistent efforts of leading scholars during the past forty years.

Major typological, liturgical, and iconographical questions affecting medieval developments have been elucidated.[1] Of even greater importance has been the increasing recognition of the over-all artistic unity of the Late-Antique–Early-Christian world. The occasionally stimulating and always controversial conception of Late Antique art as a product of the interaction between "Rome" and a never wholly defined "Orient" has not withstood the test of further study. Even formal elements such as "dwarf transepts" (i.e., side rooms flanking either the aisles of basilical churches or simple halls)–until lately considered an "Eastern" characteristic–have recently been revealed as part of the earliest major church in a no lesser "Western" center than Rome (St. John in the Lateran, ca. 320).[2] The post-Justinian development of Christian architecture in East and West may differ, but such distinctions are hardly valid in the fourth and fifth century.

While the "East-West" conception is slowly fading, it has become gradually clearer that the basic tasks facing Early Christian architecture found various solutions in the many centers of Late Antiquity. The treatment of holy sites (martyria), halls for the Eucharistic synaxes as well as tombs *ad sanctos* and baptisteries, presented the basic problems. Solutions of particular importance such as Constantine's St. Peter or the Salvator basilica (St. John in the Lateran), the structures at the site of the Holy Sepulchre in Jerusalem or of the Nativity in Bethlehem, became key monuments with continued impact on the development of later architecture in all parts of the Christian world. Some early developments such as the transept–martyrium of St. Peter's underwent gradual transformation in subsequent buildings in Italy, Greece, and Asia Minor, but both the original type and its transformations survived, ever ready for further development or even revival in a "renaissance."[3]

Other primary solutions, such as those of the recently elucidated "cemetery-basilicas" of fourth-century Rome, eventually disappeared as the functions connected with their origin died out or were absorbed into other structures.[4] Buildings originally pagan, and later adopted for Christian worship, such as the Pantheon (S. Maria Rotonda), also began to influence architectural forms during the succeeding centuries.[5]

The earliest churches in the transalpine regions were invariably small. This phenomenon is in marked contrast with the monumental buildings erected in the Mediterranean area from the time of Constantine to the Justinian period. Even where early buildings on the sites of later great churches were not tiny box-like *ad corpus* chapels outside the walls like those uncovered in Bonn, Cologne, Xanten, or St. Maurice d'Agaune,[6] but large episcopal complexes in the center as in Trier, an imperial city since the days of the Tetrarchy, a reduction in size and quality is notable in Merovingian reconstructions.[7] At the same time Early Christian architectural types and techniques, particularly those common in the fifth century, penetrated into Western Europe and the British Islands from the Late Antique centers in Italy and the "East" and survived.

Centers outside of the Frankish-Burgundian-Lombard areas such as Visigothic Spain began tangible architectural production rather late. The earliest surviving building is S. Juan de Baños of 661 A.D. But relatively little work has yet been done on Early Christian remains in Spain which are indicated by both the sources and preliminary studies.[8]

Substantial evidence of Early Christian architecture in Britain also awaits discovery. The importance of England for medieval developments lies in the architectural production following the Benedictine mission of Saint Augustine of Canterbury, dispatched from Rome by Pope Gregory the Great in 596. The subsequent relationship of the Anglo-Saxons with both the continent and with Rome makes the early architecture in southeastern and central England of special interest during the eighth and ninth centuries, when Anglo-Saxon and Irish monks were the most active missionaries of Roman Catholicism in Frisia and east of the Rhine and close allies and advisers of the Carolingian rulers.[9]

The particular character of transalpine architecture up to the seventh century must be considered a result of the essentially provincial nature of this whole region, a provinciality equivalent to the Balkan and Asia Minor backwoods of the Byzantine Empire. This conclusion has to be stated with some emphasis, since theories postulating the "decadence" of Late Antique art, often combined with the idea that "barbarian" characteristics somehow mingled with the Roman-Christian heritage to give birth to medieval art, still find their way out of old handbooks into contemporary discussions.[10] The political, social, and artistic institutions of the Merovingian, Visigothic, Lombard, and Anglo-Saxon realms in the "dark ages" represent conscious if strained attempts to conform to the still living Roman tradition as maintained in the great Late Antique centers, specifically Rome, Milan, Ravenna and, particularly, Constantinople.[11] After a final show of vigor in the fourth and fifth centuries, even Rome and Milan were on the periphery: Byzantium remained the center. The papal city is not quite a Byzantine provincial capital from the later fifth to the eighth centuries, but influence from the eastern realm is strong at this time.[12] A major Italian fountainhead of this influence was the former imperial capital and naval center, Ravenna, a Byzantine outpost from the time of Justinian until the eighth century.

The progressive decline of the western episcopal cities of Late Antiquity is due to various related political and economic developments. The advent of Islam (Mohammed, d. 632) was the major historical phenomenon spurring the beginning of the medieval era in the West. The consequences of this event, particularly the gradual disappearance of Mediterranean trade and the decline of Byzantine power that it entailed, encouraged an alliance between the increasingly independent Roman papacy and the "new men" of Carolingian Frankish feudalism in the later eighth century. The culmination of this "axis" was the coronation of Charlemagne by Pope Leo III as "Roman Emperor" in the year 800. The resulting western politico-religious configuration lost little in significance or durability–(it survived until 1804)–by being somewhat vaguely constituted both vis-à-vis the still existing Roman Empire centered in Byzantium and with regard to the relationship between the worldly and ecclesiastical powers residing in Rome and Aix-la-Chapelle.

Architecture in the Carolingian lands from the eighth to the early tenth centuries presents several distinctive aspects, directly reflecting the political, religious, and cultural policy of Pepin the Short and his successors. Four keystones of this policy were: 1) establishment of the royal personality, court culture, and architecture on the model of Constantine the Great, conceived as the ideal Roman-Christian ruler; 2) introduction of the Roman liturgy in place of the Gallican as an expression of the new alliance between Rome and the Carolingian house; 3) religious conversion of the newly conquered populations in this sense by the Benedictine missions as an adjunct of military expansion into the area east of the Rhine; and 4) foundation and fostering of monasteries and episcopal sees, both in the Carolingian heartland and in the new territories as a primary means of political and cultural consolidation following military conquest and religious conversion.

Considering the dominant role of Anglo-Saxon Benedictines in the conversion of the Frisian and Saxon population since the time of Winfrid (St. Boniface, d. 755) and their importance at the Carolingian court (e.g., Alcuin of York, d. 804), it is not surprising that simple rectangular, wooden, roofed halls with narrower square or rectangular chancels similar to those of the Northumbrian group—for example, Escomb, near Durham, ca. 700 (plates 2, 3)—should have comprised the bulk of newly founded parish and abbey churches in the conquered or freshly converted territories from the Netherlands to Westphalia, Saxony, the Meuse and the upper Rhine valley (Elst in Gelderland, ca. 726; Nivelles I, seventh century; Paderborn, St. Salvator I, late eighth century; Reichenau-Mittelzell, ca. 724–46). As a structural and formal type, this group presents neither problems nor surprises. Its origins are less clear. Nivelles I, earlier than the Northumbrian churches, is a foundation under the influence of St. Amand, the Aquitanian "apostle of the Belgians." Pirmin, the founder of Reichenau-Mittelzell, may have been a Visigoth. Whether the rectangular missionary churches in the North are a "primitive" form influenced by the shadowy architecture of the prehistoric period,[13] or merely exhibit the most advanced degree of simplification possible, dispensing with even the vestiges of formal allusion to earlier prototypes, remains open to discussion. Judging from the "Roman" masonry techniques and details of the extant Northumbrian churches, the second alternative seems the more likely.[14]

In contrast, the Kentish church group of south-eastern England, founded by St. Augustine and his followers shortly after their arrival from Rome in 596 (as at Reculver: simple

12

rectangular nave cell, column chancel screen, round or polygonal apse, flanking rooms) and similar buildings in the Merovingian lands, such as St. Martin in Angers, seventh century (plate 4), form part of the international provincial architecture common to Roman and Romanized areas from Asia Minor to Western Europe since the fifth century. In their various forms they represent reduced versions of the great key buildings of the Early Christian centers from Rome to the Holy Land.

Partly or wholly vaulted variations of this type continued a flourishing though wholly "backwoods" existence in the West until well into the eleventh century (plates 4-9, 14), concentrated in the mountainous areas from northern Spain and along the rim of the Gulf of Lyon to the Alps, Savoy, Lombardy, and Tuscany. Termed, perhaps not quite accurately, *le premier art roman* by Puig i Cadafalch,[15] the relatively numerous extant examples of this group probably owe their survival to the very remoteness of the regions in which their vestiges are found. The mainstream of Carolingian and Ottonian developments passed them by. Their significance for the evolution of Romanesque architecture is no less. This architecture shall be taken up again in a later context.

Examples of this kind were built in the Carolingian heartland as well, for example the seventh- or eighth-century basilica next to the Palatine Chapel in Aachen (plate 11). In the case of the little vaulted central oratory with triple apses and a central tower at Germigny-des-Près on the Loire, built in 806 (plates 15, 16) and badly mishandled in a nineteenth-century reconstruction,[16] it may not be wholly coincidental that the builder, Bishop Theodulf of Orléans, was of Visigothic origin. But when Einhard, Charlemagne's chancellor, who was also closely connected with the emperor's major architectural efforts, built a private church on his estates at Steinbach in the Odenwald, that building also exhibited the traditional repertory of "international" elements such as dwarf transept chambers with small apses flanking a nave with side aisles.[17]

The architecture most closely associated with the Carolingian court and its papal allies presents traits indicating a conscious revival of Early Christian themes. Several stand out, major among them Old St. Peter's in Rome (plate 1).[18] Its atrium with the pine cone *cantharus*; its open roofed nave, accompanied by two aisles on either side; the great continuous transept-martyrium and the apse on either side of the *memoria* of St.

Peter; the alcoves on either side of the transept, closed off by colonnades; even secondary features such as the straight entablature over the nave colonnade or the columns between the side aisles and the transept: one or more of these became the symbolic elements identifying the prototype, sometimes radically reduced in Carolingian copies in Rome (S. Prassede, 817–24; S. Stefano degli Abbessini, 795–816) and in the North (St. Denis; Fulda, plate 18; Cologne; Seligenstadt, plate 22). It has been suggested that the propyleum-chapel (S. Maria in turri) at the front of St. Peter's atrium, dedicated to the Virgin by Pope Paul I (757–67) and flanked by the earliest dated bell tower in Italy (built by Stephan II, 752–57), may be yet another element to be included among the features which, often wholly transformed, relate Carolingian and later buildings to the great Constantinian model.[19] At the abbey of Fulda (plate 18) the documents indicate that the builder, Abbot Ratger (791–810) wanted to give St. Boniface, the "apostle of the Germans," a memorial church equivalent to that of the apostle of Rome. The transept, complete with alcoves, lies in the west, while the Carolingian atrium (recently excavated[20]) is in the east, as at St. Peter's.

In this context the so-called Torhalle should be discussed, which, almost perfectly preserved, is about all that remains above ground of the Carolingian abbey of St. Nazarius in Lorsch (plate 19). Its polychrome marble encrustation reflects a long tradition of Merovingian decorative motifs, such as those of the seventh century burial chapel in Jouarre. But the three round arches, flanked by engaged columns with composite capitals and bearing an attic story, betray the model, a Roman triumphal arch like Constantine's near the Colosseum. Both the room in the upper story, accessible by flanking stair-towers, and the significance of the structure as a whole, remain puzzling. It has been suggested that it was an entrance chapel for ceremonial receptions. Its miniature size, the jewel-like character of the encrustation, the remarkably slim entablature and the curious zigzag arches on slender Ionic pilasters reveal the brittle quality of this Carolingian "renaissance."

Before further discussion, some relevant facts concerning pre-Carolingian architecture should be considered. The term *martyrium*, object of much study in recent decades,[21] must be defined in the narrowest sense possible, that is as the immediate surroundings of a site (for instance Golgotha) or an object (as the

Holy Cross) that had witnessed, hence is a relic of the life of Christ, the Virgin, the Apostles, or of major Old Testament figures such as Abraham or Moses, witnesses *sub lege* to the truth of the Gospels. The body, tomb, and attributes of a martyr, a witness to Christ in the blood, are objects in this sense. The name is frequently applied to the enclosing building, but it remains that the architectural framework, while of primary interest to the historian, is secondary to the martyrium as a liturgical entity which may have no formal architectural setting whatever.[22] The form of the enclosing structures, if any, was derived from pagan funerary and memorial architecture (heroa, funerary basilicas, and the like). Open or enclosed, the martyrium was generally surrounded by secondary buildings used for related liturgical purposes, baptism, eucharistic service and burials *ad sanctum*. Several martyria were sometimes clustered together in one precinct, each marked by special architectural treatment and flanked by secondary buildings (Holy Sepulchre complex, Jerusalem).[23]

The buildings required for the Eucharistic service, usually but not always basilical in form, derive from a complex of pre-Constantinian sources: cult rooms of pagan mystery religions, imperial throne rooms, public and private basilicas.[23a] Beginning in the fourth century, these buildings and the structural framework of martyria were frequently fused into a single architectural unit, as at St. Peter's (plate 1). At times a martyrium and an adjacent basilica *ad corpus* were in only tenuous connection. For example, in the pre-twelfth century arrangement at S. Lorenzo fuori le mura in Rome, openings inserted in the apse of the sixth-century basilica gave access to the older catacomb martyrium in the directly adjoining hill. Whatever the solution, these "fusions" of martyrium and congregational hall were also commonly situated in the center of a cluster of satellite structures.

To make the martyria accessible to large numbers of the faithful without disturbing the services *ad martyrem* or endangering the relic, had been a major architectural and liturgical problem since the pre-Constantinian period. Although physical contact with the holy site, relic or reliquary was the desire of the worshipers, its mere proximity or visibility was sufficient. As far as the safety of the relic and general decorum were concerned, direct physical contact by the faithful was actually undesirable.[24]

While what has been characterized as the "traffic problem" by Krautheimer explains certain aspects of the surroundings of

15

Christian martyria, the desire to reconstitute translated relics in surroundings approximating those of their original site may explain the introduction of artificially created chambers or crypts, wholly or partly under the level of the adjacent or superimposed buildings. The different forms of Early Christian underground martyria prompted the development of various crypt types. The crypts were made accessible by steps which usually led down from inside the upper building. Subterranean corridors, surrounding or flanking the martyria, facilitated the smooth flow of the faithful to and around the relic.

Late in the sixth century a variation on this theme, an annular crypt, was built around the *memoria* of St. Peter in Rome, situated between the apse and transept of the Constantinian basilica (plate 1). Originally a *sub divo* memorial niche in the pre-Constantinian necropolis on the Vatican hill, part of this structure had remained visible above the pavement of the fourth century building. Now, in a curious turnabout, it was enclosed in a setting suggestive of the catacombs: a semicircular corridor, accessible from either side in front, followed the inner curve of the apse and opened into a passage which led straight back to a small chamber (*confessio*) directly behind the *memoria* of the saint. This half-underground complex was covered with slabs forming the pavement of a raised choir over the martyrium.[25]

It is not surprising that Carolingian "copies" of St. Peter's should follow this solution, as for example, SS. Petrus and Marcellinus in Seligenstadt, 820–30 (plate 22).[26] The introduction of an annular crypt added another attribute of the original. Corridor crypts of the kind illustrated on the Plan of St. Gall (plate 20) with shafts converging on a *confessio* under the forechoir, are a variant of the annular crypt form with its focus on a single martyrium chamber.

While martyrium and Eucharistic table (*altare* or *mensa*) were originally distinct in fact and significance, they were frequently brought into immediate proximity as early as the fourth century. By the seventh century this relationship was the rule in the West, but it took various forms. Where the importance of a martyrium, either *in situ* or a translated relic, made special treatment desirable, as at St. Peter's, the relic was made accessible in a *confessio* directly below the altar. Lesser relics were introduced directly under or into the body of the altar itself, as is the practice to this day.

Starting from these precedents, Carolingian architecture,

freshly attuned to the requirements of the Roman liturgy, took a new direction which must be considered decisive. Its major buildings no longer merely comprise single martyria. While the cult might focus on the sepulchre of a local saint, the main martyrium-altar was now surrounded hieratically by a galaxy of secondary martyria with relics of holy places and saints from all parts of the Christian world. The building as an architectural whole became a microcosm, in which the major sacred sites and the whole (locally relevant) calendar of martyrs, reflecting the main tenets of Christian doctrine were schematically contained.[27] It attained topical significance by the special attention paid to local saints or to relics of non-local origin which had assumed importance by their long or miraculously efficacious association with the site. We may tentatively term this new church type "compound martyrium."[28]

The gradual process of liturgical reorientation in the West with its emphasis on the Roman rite and Roman martyrs which followed the reforms of Gregory the Great, was accompanied by a shift in the concept of what a "church" was. In Rome itself, bound by tradition, corresponding architectural transformations are less evident than in the North. A wave of rededications of existing buildings to Early Christian martyrs beginning in the seventh century, accompanied by mass translations of relics from the catacombs, is the main indication of change. But it is no coincidence that a second-century building like the Pantheon with its niches and recesses, originally a *heroon* of the deified imperial family, should be rededicated in the seventh century not only to the Assumption of the Virgin, but also to All Saints.[29] The Constantinian basilica of the Saviour (St. John in the Lateran), which apparently did not contain a martyrium in its early condition and which was intended for the Eucharistic cult, was rededicated to Saints John the Baptist and Evangelist before 870.[30]

In Rome the construction of what may be the earliest hall crypt under S. Maria in Cosmedin during the papacy of Hadrian I (772–95), is an indication of the trend to the compound martyrium. This little underground chamber is divided into three aisles by two rows of three columns each, enclosed by walls containing niches subdivided by shelves, suggesting the *columbaria* tombs of the first and second centuries A.D. The crypt, evidently intended for the display of numerous relics in surroundings approximating the atmosphere of the catacombs, was

17

terminated by a transverse shaft with an apse and made accessible by a single flight of steps leading down from the nave.[31]

The evolution of both annular and simple corridor crypts during the course of the ninth and tenth centuries responds to the same necessity. At Einhard's church in Steinbach (810–20), built to house the relics of SS. Petrus and Marcellinus, obtained with difficulty and translated from Italy with due ceremony, two major shafts intersecting crosswise lead to the major *confessio* under the nave and to an altar under the main apse. Smaller secondary shafts are appended for altars under the side apses. At St. Philibert-de-Grandlieu (plate 21) three parallel shafts branch off from a main trunk gallery to form a catacomb-like network. The *confessio*, surrounded by an access corridor, might be enlarged into a hall, sometimes with inner supports, making room for multiple relic deposits, while the outer wall of the corridor was compounded with niches, apse-like protrusions or associated outer structures (rear crypts). These may be subsidiary martyria or tombs *ad sanctos* of lay or ecclesiastical patrons. Variations on these themes are found at St. Pierre-le-Vieux in Sens, Corvey (plate 35), Vreden, St. Philibert-de-Grandlieu (plate 21), St. Martin in Tours and elsewhere.[32]

All parts of Carolingian church buildings were affected by the new church conception. The nave and aisles, while undergoing no evident formal change in the early medieval period, became the site of numerous major and minor altars in hieratic arrangement as shown in one of our most important sources of information concerning Carolingian architecture, the Plan of St. Gall[33] (plate 20). The extremes of the building, however, received particular elaboration. Since the multiplication of martyria containing relics of saints and holy sites from all parts of the Christian world, "*de diversis partibus totius Christianitatis*,"[34] is at the liturgical heart of this evolving architecture, it is not surprising that the associated superstructure should comprise elements of widely scattered derivation. The east end of the abbey church of St. Riquier in Centula, as we know it from a seventeenth century engraving after an eleventh century miniature (plate 17), serves as an example: "The entire arrangement at the east end . . . (tower, transept wings, and galleries) forms a complex unit and its ancestry includes, it would seem, a number of diversified elements: the dome or tower above the High Altar (witness Koja Kalessi or the Illissos church); towered cross churches as reflected in Tomarza in Asia Minor; cross transept churches with galleries such as Hagios Demetrios in Salonica; and even the column screens that cut off the ends of the transept of Old St. Peter's in Rome."[35] To these elements might be added the rectangular or square forechoir between nave and apse, common since the fifth century (Rome: S. Lorenzo in Lucina, 432–40; Koja Kalessi in Asia Minor) or the stairtowers necessary for access to the galleries (Milan: S. Lorenzo, late fourth century; Ravenna: S. Vitale).

The accretion of martyria-altars was not confined to the eastern end of the nave. Apses were also added at the western end, following fifth and sixth century precedents (St. Maurice d'Agaune, late eighth century; Cologne Cathedral, early ninth). At Fulda (810–19) the full apparatus of St. Peter's (western transept with apse) was joined to the already existing basilica with its apse in the east. If, as seems indicated, the Plan of St. Gall is not only a specific project for that abbey, but a generally applicable scheme for any well-appointed monastery or bishop's church (plate 20), a western martyrium was then considered a desirable, if not a standard feature.[36]

While all these various parts were combined in a single building, it was clear to all concerned that at least the major martyria were independent "churches." This idea is indirectly expressed in the Fulda documents: "(Baugulfus) orientale . . . templum . . . exstruxit . . . Ratgar sapiens architectus occidentale templum . . . mira arte et immensi magnitudine alteri copulans, unam fecit aecclesiam."[37]

Another kind of west "church" was developed within the framework of Carolingian compound martyria (plates 33, 36, 37). Over a vaulted ground floor, supported by columns or piers, rose an upper structure, open towards the nave through arcades. This upper floor was sometimes surrounded on three sides by aisles bearing a gallery. The upper room and galleries were accessible through stairtowers while the nave could be entered through the ground floor. The whole arrangement, topped by a tower, presented a massive complement to the complex of elements at the eastern end. Structures of this kind (or variations) formed the western termination of an impressive number of major Carolingian abbeys and cathedrals.[38]

A rather detailed account and a view of such a west "church" can be seen at St. Riquier in Centula (Picardy; plate 17), but only two late Carolingian examples have survived, one at Corvey (plates 33-36), the other at Werden,[39] both mutilated and transformed. Others are known only in foundations or through documentary sources.

The function of these structures has been the subject of lively discussion for several decades. The German term *Westwerk* and the French *avant nef* are descriptively neutral but inadequate. The alternative *église porche*, though misleading, does include the concept "church." "Westwork" is now the common English term. Contemporary documents refer either to *turris* or *ecclesia*: the first fits any tall structure in the early Middle Ages; the last, as we have seen, is general enough to describe also the eastern complex, a western apse, or the entire church. A text may speak, *pars pro toto*, of "*in altare sancti . . .*" or "*ad sanctum . . .,*" both usages also common for churches as a whole.

All suggestions so far advanced concerning the function or significance of westworks: parish church, baptistery, seat of judgment, fortress—symbolic or operational, mausoleum, royal chapel or loggia in imitation of Aachen (cf. below), remain hypothetical. Early medieval sources throw remarkably little definitive light on this question.

According to the indications given by Angilbert and Hariulf in their description of St. Riquier (plate 17), laymen pertaining to the abbey as well as monks and novices received communion at Easter and Christmas during mass in the Salvator (upper west) church. The men and women were separated, apparently in the aisles, while the novices were in the galleries. On the following days, however, mass was said for both monks and laymen ("*omnes*") both in the eastern part of the church ("*ad Sanctum Richarium*") and in the Mary chapel near by ("*ad Sanctam Mariam*"), but without communion. While mass for the parish was sometimes read in the westwork, it was apparently not the parish church. The distribution of the choirs of monks and novices on various holidays may be similarly understood. One of the choirs was sometimes "*ad sanctum Salvatorem*," but not always. The westwork was not a "choir loft." Nor is the nature and function of the vaulted ground floor below much clearer. Angilbert reports that a casket containing relics of the Virgin and numerous female martyrs was placed "*subtus cryptam Sancti Salvatoris*." No altar is mentioned. During the processional liturgy, a station was repeatedly made "*in paradysum coram sanctam Nativitatem*," immediately after entering the atrium and before proceeding either "*ad sanctum Salvatorem*" or "*ad sanctum Richarium*." There was a plaster image of the Nativity

20

near the portal of the "crypta"—which may mean vaulted, but not necessarily subterranean.

In numerous pre-mid-century examples the westwork appears to be a later addition to an already existing building. At St. Liudger in Werden, for example, the sources, if wholly reliable, indicate that the abbey was also a parish church and the seat of the synodal court as early as 875. The Werden westwork, dedicated to St. Mary, was not consecrated until 943, however, and perhaps not begun before the tenth century. Hence it was apparently not required for either of these or for other basic liturgical functions.[40]

There is a less defined pattern of Carolingian westwork *patrocinia* than is sometimes implied. The westworks at Reims Cathedral, Fontanella, and Centula were dedicated to the Saviour, while those at St. Germain in Auxerre and, perhaps, Corvey contained altars of St. John. At Werden, the dedication is to the Virgin Mary, at Halberstadt there was an upper altar of St. Sixtus, and so on. The picture is no less varied in the case of double apses: Cologne—St. Peter and St. Mary; Fulda—St. Boniface and St. Salvator; Plan of St. Gall—St. Peter and St. Paul with St. Gall in the forechoir. The pattern in post-Carolingian westworks and double apses, even if relevant, is no more revealing.

It would seem that westworks and second—usually western —apses (sometimes with a transept as at St. Peter's) are variations on the same theme. Both are frequently additions to already existing buildings (Fulda, Werden, Corvey, Fontanella, and elsewhere); both contain one or more reliquary altars; both are called "ecclesia" and serve as "stations" in the processional liturgy. The acquisition of additional important relics, a concern of royalty, nobility and prelates, would provide sufficient reason for the creation of a second major martyrium compound of either kind at a still unelaborated end of the nave, as for example in Fulda.

21

This problem is still pending, but the very elusiveness of the early sources would seem to be an important clue. Further study may show that the westworks, like other "churches" architecturally linked in the framework of medieval compound martyria, have various liturgical functions and significance, perhaps in part related to their dedication, that is the relics they contain.

The Palace Chapel of Charlemagne at Aachen (Aix-la-Chapelle) remains the major surviving monument of Carolingian architecture (plates 11-13). Built from about 790 on and dedicated in 805 by Pope Leo III, it deserves close study, for its own sake as well as because it has been suggested as the "key" to the west-work question.[41]

The two arcades and the inner octagon's clerestory are covered by an eight-sided cloister vault and surrounded by an ambulatory supporting a gallery. A degree of complication is introduced into the spatial development of the ambulatory and gallery by the sixteen-sided outer wall of the chapel. Interpenetrating triangular and four-partite groin vaults span the ambulatory. The gallery is covered by alternating rectangular and triangular barrel vaults which rise to buttress the vault of the octagon. The gallery faces the interior through a double tier of Corinthian columns set into the upper arches surrounding the octagon. Like other formal aspects of the chapel, original marble revetments, mosaic decoration (both replaced by modern details), and the bronze balustrades are elements evolving from the architectural repertory of Late Antiquity. The structural achievement at Aachen negates the still common suggestion that the evident lack of vaulting in most Carolingian and Ottonian architecture is due to technical difficulties. The answer must be sought elsewhere, namely in the continued reference to certain pre-Carolingian models. To vault or not to vault was not really a technical question. The decision often depended on the prototypes vaulted or not as the case may be.

At the same time, Aix-la-Chapelle is a building "of its own time." Although the clear definition of its component parts is now perhaps overly accentuated by the loss of the original marble and mosaic encrustation, a comparison with buildings from the Justinian period such as S. Vitale in Ravenna or the Hagia Sophia in Constantinople reveals characteristic differences. The Palace Chapel in Aachen is not only smaller than S. Vitale, still commonly cited as a model for Charlemagne's chapel, it also lacks the sixth-century building's spatial complication. It shares with contemporary architecture of both the "international provincial" and the "Early Christian Renaissance" trends a tendency to smallness combined with solidity. Its "Antique" elements have a brittle quality comparable with the decoration of the Lorsch Torhalle.

Mere reference to S. Vitale is insufficient in putting Aachen into perspective. As in other Carolingian compound martyria, multiple levels of form and meaning have been combined which result in a new unit of considerable complexity. The building is dedicated to both the Virgin and the Saviour. Contemporary

22

sources describe the whole complex of palace chapel, *regia*, and courtyard with porticoes as a "Nova Roma" or as the "Lateran." This characterization is reinforced by the report that Charlemagne brought an equestrian statue, probably of Theodoric the Great, back from his Italian campaigns, to be erected in the court of the palace as an equivalent to such monuments in Constantinople and Rome (specifically, the equestrian statue of Marcus Aurelius which stood near the Lateran palace in Rome throughout the Middle Ages, surviving because it was believed to be that of Constantine the Great). It should be recalled in this connection that the Lateran basilica, perhaps Constantine's palace church in Rome, was also originally dedicated to the Saviour and that the fifth-century baptistery near it is an octagonal building not wholly unlike the Aachen chapel.

The throne of Charlemagne in the western bay of the gallery originally looked down to the altar of the Virgin in the eastern bay of the ambulatory and across to the altar of the Saviour in the gallery above it. In the cupola Christ was represented enthroned with the Elders and Beasts of the Apocalypse (Rev. 4:4-8; 5:6-8), a symbol of divine world government. This is the only mosaic representation of those originally in the building which is securely documented, though it too is now no longer in its original condition. Krautheimer has suggested the seventh-century Hagios Soros chapel in the Blachernae Palace in Constantinople, known only through written sources, as a possible point of reference within the context of "Sancta Maria Rotonda."[5] It contained relics of the Virgin similar to those preserved at Aachen, perhaps also had a royal loge.[42]

The oratory was eventually destined to become Charlemagne's tomb and its formal relationship with such Late Antique mausolea as Constantine's next to the Apostoleion in Constantinople, Theodoric's in Ravenna, S. Constanza in Rome and, last but not least, the Holy Sepulchre rotunda in Jerusalem, made it wholly suitable for that purpose. The Apocalyptic representation in the dome might even form a point of contact with St. Peter's in Rome, on whose façade the same scene was featured during the later Middle Ages and, perhaps, earlier.

Many problems remain. Where, for instance, were the many relics kept? What was the function of the large room in the western tower behind the throne or of the room above it? Were relics displayed from there to be seen from the atrium below as has been suggested?[43]

It is still too early to draw a final balance of this glittering spectrum of formal, iconographical, and liturgical elements. It may be, however, that the particular combination at Aachen has specific relevance to the historic event of the imperial coronation in St. Peter's on Christmas Day of the year 800.

The imperial ideal and the precarious balance of church and state which were the ideological foundations of the Carolingian Empire, survived the disintegration of that loosely constituted realm. The Carolingian policy of cultural and political consolidation through imperial abbeys and episcopal sees was continued by the Ottonian successors. The education of Saxonian princes and princesses was provided in abbeys and convents frequently headed by members of the royal family. Imperial bishops like Notker of Liège, Egbert of Trier, Willigis of Mainz, Tietmar of Merseburg and, not least, Bernward of Hildesheim, were at the very center of Ottonian cultural and political life. Gerbert of Reims as Silvester II led the young Otto III to a palace on the Aventine, to dreams of a reconstituted Constantinian empire, and to an early death.

The Carolingians were not unaware of the imperial capital on the Bosporus. Charlemagne is even said to have considered a personal alliance with the Empress Irene. But the orientation of the Ottonians towards Byzantium was much stronger. The great revival of power and culture of the Eastern empire under the Macedonian dynasty in the tenth century made Byzantine art and customs once again the imperial model to be emulated. Ottonian embassies in Constantinople under Liutprand of Cremona weathered Byzantine intrigues and haughtiness to achieve cordial relations. The chief result of their labors and the symbolic culmination of this medieval effort at East-West understanding was the marriage of Otto II to one of the lesser princesses of the Byzantine court, Theophanu, in 972.

Medieval architecture is a changing blend of "survivals" and "revivals," composed into new and original solutions. An evaluation of any building in this period depends upon a careful analysis in which the various ingredients are weighed and distinguished. Ottonian architecture begins with the characteristic features of Carolingian art—a survival of "international provincial" architecture; and a revival of major "themes" of Early Christian architecture. To these are added two further components, a revival of Carolingian motifs, and the introduction of elements from recent and contemporary architecture in the Byzantine realm.

The symbolic import of Constantine's St. Peter's had not lost its meaning around the year 1000. There are few major abbeys or cathedrals of this time which do not contain some fragmentary reflection of the great model, if only minor transformed details, as at Mainz, Strasbourg, Regensburg, Augsburg, Mittelzell (plates 44-46), Schaffhausen, Aquileia, Montecassino (plate 63), and Ripoll (plates 58, 59).

St. Croix in Orléans, St. Remi in Reims, and St. Bertin at St. Omer, all built in the first half of the eleventh century, represent a group in northern France which turns to another important Early Christian type (Hagios Demetrios in Salonica) with aisles and, sometimes, also galleries, extending around a transept.[44] Pisa (plates 98-100) has related antecedents.

The revival of Carolingian motifs has similar significance. The figure of Charlemagne had assumed a stature equal to Constantine's in the Ottonian age. The Saxons received the royal crown in Aachen. Otto III is said to have opened Charlemagne's tomb and he was buried there. The implications of this Carolingian revival are most obviously expressed in a series of "copies" of Aix-la-Chapelle, for example Mettlach, Nimwegen, Ottmarsheim, Groningen, Muizen, and Essen.[45]

It is difficult to determine when the components of Ottonian buildings are survivals of the indestructible international provincial architecture, spread across southern Europe since the fifth century, or fresh imports from the Byzantine sphere. One might ask if there is any difference at all, since the new elements are but fresh shoots, cut closer to the still flourishing trunk of a tree, transplants of which had long struck roots in the West. But while the old transplants reproduced their own kind with the immutable sturdiness of the provincial, the architecture of the Eastern realm underwent the gradual evolution which characterizes all living art. Relative proximity to the active Eastern metropolis is important in this context, since Ottonian architecture has less direct resemblance to contemporary buildings in Byzantium itself than to the architecture of its provinces, particularly that of the then recently subdued Bulgarian empire.

The convent church of St. Cyriacus in Gernrode (Saxony)[46] (plates 23, 24) was begun by the Margrave Gero in 963 and perhaps completed under the auspices of the Empress Theophanu after 972. Its continuous transept with side apses, forechoir and

25

apse as well as a westwork with flanking stairtowers are a blend of Carolingian and international provincial features. But the arcaded galleries and alternating pier and column supports, dividing nave and aisles below, introduce an element of color, rhythm and complication original with Byzantine churches like Hagios Demetrios in Salonica and still found in ninth and tenth century buildings in the Bulgarian provinces, as in Mesembria and Aboba Pliska.[47]

With the exception of the major eastern and western parts, the architectural definition of the individual martyria in Carolingian buildings was quite minimal. Secondary altars were disposed in the nave, side aisles, and transept arms of the church in the St. Gall plan (plate 20) without receiving particular architectural attention. The same seems to be true of the various subsidiary westwork altars. Some of the complications of Ottonian architecture may be due to the pure delight in decorative and formal refinements of a cultivated upper class of royal and ecclesiastical patrons. Yet one might also suggest that the rich but subtly modulated combination of articulating and spatial elements, derived from Early Christian, international provincial, Carolingian and contemporary Byzantine sources, such as blind arcades, corbel friezes, niches, and diaphragm arches, as at Nivelles (plate 40), and Hildesheim (plates 29-32), served to differentiate the previously unarticulated parts comprising compound martyria.

Ottonian architecture was not merely eclectic. It absorbed something of the synthetic qualities of Byzantine art illustrated by the blending of longitudinal and central elements characterizing Eastern architecture since the sixth century. The western tower of St. Maria of Mittelzell on the Reichenau is not just a kind of simplified westwork flanked by passages leading from the west transept to an atrium. It also contains an apse merged, unsuspected, within it, as if to suggest the liturgical identity of westwork and west apse (plates 44-46).

The wholly preserved western end of the abbey of the church in Essen (first half of the eleventh century; plates 25-28) is a classic example of Ottonian "interpenetration." Reading from inside out, we find three sides of a hexagon on piers, arcaded as in Aix-la-Chapelle, but covered with a domical pendentive vault. This hexagon is set into the lower part of a square tower with beveled corners flanked by octagonal stair turrets. The resulting "ambulatory" is covered by interpenetrating three-partite and four-partite groin vaults. Unlike Aachen, the gallery above is covered by triangular and square groin vaults. The diaphragm arches between the gallery bays are penetrated by small openings with Ionic colonettes and enclose tiny triangular secondary galleries accessible from the stairtowers. Rising from this complex of interlocking spaces, the upper octagonal tower emerges, partially resting on squinches. It is pierced by arched bifora openings and topped by a conical roof. The rest of the church with western and eastern transepts of various sizes and heights, circular apse with polygonal outer faces, niches along the side walls and in the main transept, and an adjoining tripartite rear crypt, matches the complex refinement of the western end. There is nothing just like this in the Byzantine capital. The now almost wholly ruined Myrelaion church (939)[48] is similarly sophisticated, but simpler in contour and elevation and, though vaulted and buttressed, almost fragile by comparison.

If articulation can lead to complexity, it can also serve to clarify. Yet the element of clarity should not be exaggerated at St. Michael in Hildesheim,[48a] early eleventh century (plates 29-32). One wonders, for example, whether the crossing created by the intersection of the equally high nave and transept, segregated by four diaphragm arches of equal height, is not the result of a characteristically Ottonian "merger" between a continuous transept and a tripartite transept with lower side arms. The crossing squares at either end at Hildesheim are not the "measure" of the building. The transept galleries with their superimposition of arcades; the opposition of a triapsidal eastern end with a narrow forechoir to the western complex; the choir with the apse raised high over a hall crypt surrounded by a barrel-vaulted ambulatory with wall niches: these elements are as variegated as those at Essen. The use of polychrome masonry, alternation of supports, blind arcades and niches enhances the "Ottonian" effect.

Recent studies demonstrate that this kind of architecture extends far beyond the rather vague medieval boundary lines of the Ottonian realm.[49] Similar tendencies may be observed in most of the architecture north of the Loire in the Meuse valley (Nivelles, plate 40), the Champagne (as in the nave of Vignory, plate 54, enlivened by the bifora of a false gallery and a diaphragm arch with penetrations), and as far south as Italy (Pisa, 1063 f., plates 98, 100, with galleries in the nave and transept arms and colorful marble encrustation). In Normandy the penetration of

27

the walls by galleries figured as an element of rhythmic articulation from the tenth century on (St. Pierre in Jumièges).[50]

It is unfortunate that our conception of early eleventh-century architecture must be based on so few surviving examples. The apparent simplicity of the ruin of Limburg on the Hardt (plates 41-43), founded by Konrad II in 1025 and entrusted to the reform abbot Poppo of Stablo,[51] contrasts with the complex colors and forms of Saxon, lower Rhenish and Mosan churches of this period. But much of the effect may be due to the loss of most of the original details and plaster. With the original crossing tower and probable reduced westwork flanked by turrets, the ensemble was surely much richer. Yet a certain clarification of surfaces and spaces by diaphragm arches and blind arcades is notable at Limburg. The articulation of the choir (plate 42) and the mathematical division of the hall crypt below into three-by-three groin-vaulted bays on columns with cubic capitals constitutes a new, simpler language based on idioms used in more complex fashion elsewhere.

L'an mil and the century that followed it was not only a time of imperial nostalgia and byzantinizing refinement, but also of apocalyptic fears, asceticism, and an ecclesiastic reform which eventually led to a break between the German emperors and the papacy.[52] Something of all this is reflected in both Limburg and the great imperial cathedral of Speyer I (plates 48-50), begun by Konrad II and built about 1030–60.[53] Its rectangular westwork with octagonal tower, the two towers on either side of the nave, the chancel and the crossing tower are developments of themes sounded in Centula, Hildesheim, and Essen. The hall crypt, containing the tombs *ad sanctos* of the Salian dynasty, is similar to that at Limburg and novel mainly because of its enormous extent under the whole transept and choir. But simplicity was combined with monumental size at Speyer I. As at Limburg, the only exterior ordering elements were pilaster strips with corbel friezes and arched window openings. The interior too was restrained: nave and clerestory wall on square piers, articulated by blind arcades on shaft-like engaged columns; side aisles with groin vaults; the nave unvaulted; cubic capitals throughout.

Norman architecture in the age of William the Conqueror, while working with a somewhat different vocabulary, arrived at a language of similar clarity, simplicity, and forcefulness. Mont-Saint-Michel, about 1060 (plate 70), bears the hallmarks: bay

28

division by engaged column shafts rising from the ground to an open roof (the present wooden barrel vault is modern); and clear demarcation of parts. The archivolts of the nave arcade are distinguished from the clerestory wall and rest on separate engaged columns; blind arches are incised around the clerestory windows as at Speyer I; the aisles are groin vaulted. Galleries are characteristic for Normandy, however after 1040 the gallery openings are no longer an element of color and rhythm as at Gernrode, Vignory or St. Pierre in Jumièges, but of articulation. That they need have no other "practical" function is clear at Mont-Saint-Michel where the gallery is "blind," that is, the gallery arcades open into the unlit space under the aisle roof. Notre Dame at Jumièges (ca. 1040–67)[54] (plates 55-57) is comparable, but the galleries are accessible, lit by windows, groin vaulted and divided into slightly rectangular bays by strong transverse arches like the aisles below. The subdivision of the unvaulted nave into square units is emphasized by the alternation of supports with high rising engaged shafts. As Ernst Gall observed, this is an architecture conceived in clearly articulated layers of functioning masonry and space.[55] Nave, aisles, and galleries are juxtaposed and superimposed spatial shafts, organized into easily comprehensible blocks by a skeletal system of supporting and buttressing elements. Inert wall as a filling element is largely eliminated. The active masonry itself becomes "readable," being composed of large, carefully hewn ashlars as at Speyer. Decorative details including Corinthian capitals, are severely schematized. The plan of the eastern end, suggested by excavations, resembles the recently clarified arrangement at St. Michael in Hildesheim, but there is no crypt. The massive square towers flanking the simplified westwork have assumed a size and importance far beyond that of their Carolingian and Ottonian antecedents which had always been outweighed by a great central westwork tower. At Jumièges they rise well above the central block as independent units, perhaps for the first time in the medieval period. This motif became standard in Greater Normandy (including England after 1066) as in the definitive solution at St. Etienne in Caen after 1068 (plate 69).

The architectural problem of the compound martyrium posed by liturgical evolution was faced in the Carolingian period and given some basic solutions: compound crypts, compound eastern groupings, double apses, westworks, and/or west towers, nave and aisles with multiple altars. Ottonian refinements led to

29

subtle distinctions and complex interrelationships between the liturgically independent, but architecturally coherent parts. But the main line of Western medieval development lay in the way of simplification and clarification. The meaning of the whole, composed of distinct, schematically related parts, was to become comprehensible at a glance, reflecting the essentially simple social, political and ideological order of feudal Europe. With Speyer I, Notre-Dame-de-Jumièges, and related churches,[56] medieval architecture in the old Lotharingia, comprising Holland, Belgium, northern France, the Rhineland, and extending over the Alps to Italy, had entered its definitive phase: it had become "Romanesque."

While architecture in the North underwent its complex development, meeting and solving the challenges presented by an evolving social order, the *premier art roman* of the southern ring from Spain to the Alps continued on its somnolent way, building small, dark, very solid, partly or wholly vaulted churches with buttresses, triple apses, small crossing towers, dwarf transepts, massive piers, external pilaster strip and corbel frieze articulation with niches under the apse eaves. The buildings evidence a crude, but structurally effective masonry technique, reminiscent of the Late Antique traditions[57] from which all this architecture had sprung and which, in its mountain retreats, it had nurtured and preserved. St. Peter in Mistail, Grisons, probably early ninth century (plate 14), S. Cristina de Lena in Asturia, early tenth century (plates 5-7), and St. Martin in Canigou in the French Pyrenees, early eleventh century (plates 37-39), represent this type. St. Maria in Ripoll Catalonia, late tenth–early eleventh century (plates 58, 59), is of the same family, but somewhat unusual in that its plan à la St. Peter's represents an influence from the sphere of church reform. (Its present polished state including the vaults is the result of over-restoration early in this century.) S. Pietro in Agliate near Milan (plates 8-9) has long been assigned a ninth-century date. But its hall crypt, which does not appear to be a later addition, and an overall correspondence with better dated buildings such as St. Martin at Aime (Savoy) and St. Maurice in Amsoldingen (Switzerland), seem to indicate that it was also built in the first quarter of the eleventh century.[58]

The *premier art roman* began to rejoin the mainstream of European developments when it furnished the means of architectural expression to the Order of Cluny.[59] The history of Western monasticism is a history of reforms. Those of the Carolingian era (such as the Council of Aachen in 817), prepared the Benedictines for their cultural and religious mission in the service of an empire whose worldly and spiritual heads had few conflicts of interest. The order did its job well, but the autonomy of the abbeys and the weakness of the papacy in the succeeding centuries combined to make the abbots and the imperial bishops —mostly Benedictines or graduates of the abbey schools—into trusted arms of Ottonian policy. Medieval idealism and anti-imperial politics soon combined in the formation of a reform order stressing ritual observance, monastic discipline, popular as opposed to courtly religiosity, and primary loyalty to the Church and its head in Rome. Its highly centralized organization with a single supreme abbey and a multitude of dependent priories and parishes in France, Northern Spain, Italy, and the Alps was bound to give the architectural form of the mother church some importance.

To an extent, the location of the order in Cluny was an accident of history, but its pivotal position between Aquitaine, the northern ring of France, and the Empire was significant, since Burgundian builders were exposed to influences from all architectural trends current in the tenth and eleventh centuries.

The first large abbey church built at Cluny in the second half of the tenth century, Cluny II (plates 51, 52), as known through Professor Conant's studies, with its broad horseshoe apse, side-apse niches, side chambers (*cryptae*), dwarf transept arms, crossing tower and barrel vaulting, follows in the tradition of what Porter called "Gulf of Lyon architecture." But the grouping of altars in the apses at the eastern end, in the transept arms and in the nave as well as the forechurch with its towers and the atrium, reflect the evolution of monastic architecture in the Carolingian-Ottonian heartland. The reform liturgy as set down in the eleventh century Cluniac *Consuetudines* states that the laymen should stand "under the towers" of the "galilee" (probably on an upper level) "*ut non impediant processionem.*" A relationship with Carolingian westworks is evident.

The originality of Cluniac forms should not be exaggerated. St. Philibert in Tournus (Burgundy),[60] not a Cluniac abbey, is similar in character. It is not the nature and origin of the elements, but the combination of the evolved and articulated Carolingian-Ottonian compound martyrium with the provincial

31

tradition of massive vaulting and buttressing in the area of the *premier art roman*, which gives Cluny II and related Burgundian architecture its significance. When these two early medieval strains with their rich possibilities of development had combined, Romanesque architecture was ready for its final phase.

The century-and-a-half from 1050 to 1200 was a time of change. The German emperors, steadily weakened by the growing concessions to be paid for the fidelity of their own feudal retainers, were increasingly opposed by an ever stronger papacy, sustained by the international arm of reformed Benedictine monasticism (Cluny, Hirsau, Vallombrosa, Montecassino) and allied with the rising bourgeoisie of the Italian cities. The Capetian and Norman rulers of France and England faced similar problems, but the French crown soon seized its opportunity for an alliance with the growing power of the banker, merchant and artisan class in the cities, revived by the gradual restoration of European manufacture and commerce in the eleventh century.[61] The social, political, and religious pressures generated by the slow decline of feudalism, the rapid ascendency of the towns and the rising prestige of the papacy found an outlet in the successive crusades beginning in the later eleventh century. With the treasures of the East beckoning, with the south of Italy and Sicily open for the taking, conflict in the heart of Europe was postponed for over a century. It was a time for diplomacy, not bloodletting. Armies were heavy but small, battles few, armed sieges, armed stalemates, and armed negotiation frequent. Henry IV's trip to Canossa in 1077 is but a well publicized incident among many. Princes and prelates were in almost continuous motion across the continent on affairs of church and state. Romanesque culture is, consequently, an international culture. Its literary, liturgical, and diplomatic language, Latin, gave an intellectual unity to a restricted, well-educated upper class from the Baltic Sea to the tip of Italy.

While the patrons of Romanesque architecture moved on a high international plane, the actual builders were considerably less mobile. True enough, groups of artisans did travel about in the retinue of patrons, and groups of journeymen did wander in search of work. But it is the combination of an international culture with the ingrained traditions of local craftsmanship which gave Romanesque architecture in the different regions of Europe its varying complexion.[62]

Norman architecture entered its High Romanesque phase with all the means required, but vaulting, the touchstone of "progress" in past discussions, did not put in an appearance before about 1100 (choirs of St. Trinité in Caen, and Durham Cathedral). St. Etienne in Caen (ca. 1064–87), the definitive building of this period and a personal foundation of William the Conqueror, worked with an elevation similar to that developed at Jumièges. A narrow arcaded triforium gallery formed yet another juxtaposed spatial shaft in front of the clerestory windows while engaged columns marked a rhythmic change of support in the nave. At Cérisy-la-Forêt (ca. 1070–80, transformed in the nineteenth century) similarly engaged shafts articulated the nave walls, but a diaphragm arch, rising from each second pier, subdivided the nave into rectangular units.

The diaphragm arch, engaged shafts, and alternating supports as key features of Romanesque spatial organization appeared at the same time in Lombardy (S. Maria Maggiore in Lomello), and in Tuscany (S. Pier Scheraggio and S. Miniato in Florence).

S. Miniato (ca. 1070 f.)[63] (plates 71-73), like so much of medieval architecture in central Italy, still breathes an aroma of Early Christian Antiquity: arcades on columns with Antique or "antiquizing" capitals, mosaics, marble encrustation, open roof, gabled façade. On closer examination it proves to be no less "Romanesque" than the Norman churches. The apparatus of Antique membering and decoration articulates the building into independent geometrical components rather than into its organically functioning parts in the classical tradition. Instead of organic coherence, we have clarity through schematization. The division into three equal units by diaphragm arches on engaged columns, the blind arcades in the apse, the geometrical patterns of the encrustation: these elements speak a clear medieval language.

Three successive periods can be distinguished in the façade (ca. 1100, 1150, and 1200): simple rectangles below, more complex diagonal patterns above. The portals are not set into a classical jamb and lintel system, but completely surrounded by their marble frames and abstracted into the total geometrical design of the façade. The organic system of the upper story is literally "disorganized" by the "bent" architraves which group the pilasters into incoherent pairs. They combine with the wheel and rectangle patterns within them to form rectangular units with an abstract life of their own.

33

Nothing could demonstrate more concretely the "dissonance" of arbitrarily juxtaposed formal patterns characterizing medieval artistic method than the total lack of relationship between the systems of support in the nave and crypt of S. Miniato. Whatever logic determined the spacing of the crypt colonnettes, no possible arrangement could avoid a conflict with the foundations of the choir columns penetrating through the crypt vaults.[64] But "incoherence" should not be interpreted as "insignificance." The meaning of medieval abstractions, whether graphic or architectural, is contained not in the parts, but in the complex totality of the pattern itself. Inherent "faults" such as those of S. Miniato remain a part of architectural theory and practice as late as the sixteenth century.[65]

Speyer was rebuilt after about 1080[66] (plates 48-50). Each alternate nave pier was strengthened and subdivided by a wide intermediate capital. The resulting double bays were covered with high rising domical groin vaults. Transept, crossing, and apse were wholly rebuilt over the old crypt. The apse exterior was given rhythmic organization by blind arcades on engaged colonnette shafts. Dwarf galleries, a striking new motif of articulation in depth, perhaps developed from the eave niches common in both Ottonian architecture (Hersfeld, Xhignesse[67]) and the *premier art roman* (Agliate, Aime), run along under the roof line of the nave, transept and apse, ascending and descending along the pitch of the choir gable.

The decorative treatment of the windows and colonnette capitals at Speyer II is so similar to late eleventh-century decoration in Lombardy, that a close architectural relationship between these regions is beyond doubt. But it is not surprising that the gateway to the Italian peninsula should be exposed also to influences from Normandy and southern France. The trefoil plan of S. Fedele in Como[68] reflects similar lower Rhenish plans (S. Maria im Kapitol, Cologne[69]), but the elevation with groin-vaulted aisles and galleries and an open roofed nave divided by diaphragm arches resembles contemporary Norman solutions.

S. Ambrogio in Milan[70] (plates 92, 93), probably begun in the last quarter of the eleventh century, is the decisive building of Lombard Romanesque. Its triapsidal plan and the niche articulation under the apse eaves are a legacy from the *premier art roman* (Agliate). Galleries and towers flanking the church (one completed in 1128, one older) may reflect Norman ideas. But the great domical vaults over the nave bays have the same effect as the groin vaults then being built over the nave of Speyer. Whatever the structural purpose of the rectangular ribs marking the diagonal groins of the Milan vaults, they further emphasize the division into easily comprehensible geometrical parts which marks this period elsewhere. The lack of a clerestory and the barrel vaulting of the forechoir relates S. Ambrogio to contemporary churches of southern and central France, such as St. Foy at Conques (plate 47). The hall crypt parallels that of Speyer.

The Modena Cathedral[71] (plates 74, 75), begun about 1120 with an interior elevation marked by change of support, diaphragm arches, and false galleries (Vignory, plate 54), a hall crypt under the choir and a triapsidal exterior with blind arcades and dwarf galleries, again demonstrates the confluence in Lombardy of architectural ideas current in various parts of Europe. Its dwarf transept arms and nave vaults are later additions. Exterior elements appearing at Pisa (plate 99) in the second quarter of the twelfth century, such as blind arcades and dwarf galleries, are in a similar idiom.

The influence of the church reform inspired by Cluny was felt in Italy too. At S. Abbondio in Como (plate 76) a new Benedictine church was dedicated by the Cluniac pope Urban II in 1095. Its open roofed nave with double side aisles mirrors old St. Peter's as well as the contemporary Cluny III (cf. below and plate 53). It has no transept, but a long forechoir and four side apses required by the reform liturgy. The bell towers over the side apses indicate a connection with the reform monasteries of the Hirsau group in Swabia, Thuringia and Switzerland.[72] A two-storied "galilee," originally in front of the façade, is in the same tradition.

Montecassino[73] was rebuilt during the abbacy of Desiderius (after 1066), who followed Gregory VII to the papal throne as Victor III in 1086. The allegiance of the reformers to the throne of St. Peter's is expressed by the plan with a great continuous transept and an atrium (plate 63). Montecassino was altered in the seventeenth century, but such a transept with triple apses over a hall crypt is preserved at the Salerno Cathedral, 1077 f. (plate 64).

Romanesque elements from Campania, Lombardy, Normandy, and the Rhineland appear in the three successive building phases of S. Nicola in Bari (plates 65-67), begun in 1089, shortly after the Norman knights under Robert Guiscard had seized this and the other Apulian cities from the last remaining Byzantine garrisons in southern Italy (1071 f.).[73a] The first plan was for an open roofed church like in Montecassino or Salerno, with a great hall crypt under the transept and a high basilical nave on an arcaded colonnade. The transept of Trani, after 1097 (plate 68), and the nave of Taranto (1071 f.) reflect this combination. In its second period, about 1110, the side aisles were groin vaulted, galleries built over them, and the nave divided into two equal parts of three bays each by an engaged column shaft rising from a cruciform pier in the center. A second tower was added opposite an already existing tower flanking the west façade. The building, in short, was "medievalized" according to the Norman canon. Beginning about 1120, dwarf galleries were added over the arcaded niches articulating the exterior wall of the side aisles, built during the preceding phase. A kind of "eastwork" behind the transept with flanking towers and an octagonal tower on squinches over the crossing were begun, but left incomplete. The intended grouping of towers and the dwarf galleries must be compared with Speyer II.

In France church reform provided the stimulus for a wave of eleventh-century building south of the Loire. Cluny II was remarkable, less for new plan features than for the combination of the Carolingian-Ottonian tradition with the legacy of the *premier art roman*. What was only tentatively articulated at Cluny II, became clearly expressed in Cluny III, begun in 1088 when the reform movement was at its crest (plates 51-53). The basic features are similar: barrel-vaulted nave, elaborate choir, and a west church with towers. New is the enormous size, the double transept and the massing of towers at both ends, comparable to Speyer. The choir arrangement, that is forechoir and apse, opening through an arcade into a barrel-vaulted ambulatory, surrounded by a ring of apsidal chapels is a monumental development of earlier ambulatory forms (Vreden, St. Martin in Tours, Hildesheim). The clear expression of parts that this solution permits is essentially Romanesque. Transverse arches under the pointed barrel vault of the nave play a role similar to the diaphragm arches of Normandy and Italy. Strongly "antiquizing" in character, the details, capitals, and moldings parallel similar tendencies in the Tuscan "Protorenaissance." Both the dedication of the church to the Apostles Peter and Paul and the four-aisled plan with a great transept follow a by then well-established symbolic tradition. The second smaller transept, a novelty, found later echoes in English abbeys and cathedrals similarly populated by large chapters of monks and canons.

With Cluny, known mainly through Professor Conant's valuable reconstructions, the nearby Cluniac priory of Paray-le-Monial, ca. 1100 (plates 60-62), with similar features serves as an illustration. St. Lazare in Autun, ca. 1120 f., (plate 10), combines the triapsidal plan of Cluny II with an elevation developed from Cluny III. The details are even more strongly *all'antica* derived from sources in the ample ruins of Burgundy and the Provence. Monumental sculpture again became a part of architecture in the later eleventh century. At Autun, as at Cluny and elsewhere in Burgundy, it is concentrated on the tympanum over the nave portal. That Cluniac forechurches are closely related to earlier westworks is nowhere more clearly demonstrated than at the priory church of St. Marie-Madeleine in Vézelay,[74] ca. 1090–1130, (plates 90, 91). As in the westwork of St. Pantaleon in Cologne (ca. 1000), there is no ground floor crypt. The central room is surrounded by aisles and galleries. While the figured capitals of the nave are in the Burgundian manner of ca. 1100, the elevation of the Madeleine suggests another side of Burgundian Romanesque, namely the influence of contemporary Rhenish solutions (as the Benedictine abbey of Maria Laach, built after 1093) combined with the coloristic Ottonian tradition.

Fine regional distinctions are nowhere less conducive to an understanding of Romanesque phenomena than in the south-central area comprising the Nivernais, the Auvergne, and the Languedoc. While the major churches throughout this area have barrel vaulted naves, usually without clerestories, groin vaulted aisles, half-barrel-vaulted galleries, and "Cluniac" choirs, two main architectural approaches may be discerned.

A first group utilizes elements similar to those of Normandy-Burgundy, leading to schematic clarification of component parts. The language of the plastic details is, on the whole, less markedly *alla maniera antica* than in Burgundy, but no less colorful in its highly stylized variety. St. Etienne in Nevers (plates 87-89), a Cluniac priory of ca. 1060 f., is an almost classic illustration of this blend of southern and northern traditions. Except for the introduction of barrel vaults the elevation is a cross between Jumièges and Mont-Saint-Michel. The choir end with ambulatory and radiating absidioles parallels Cluny III. Even the pierced diaphragm arches subdividing the dwarf transept arms clarify rather than complicate the interior space. Its capitals are an extreme stereometric simplification of the Corinthian prototype. The exterior articulation is likewise simple and clear, employing a sober minimum of traditional elements surviving from international provincial architecture.

What the impetus of religious reform created architecturally for the monastic community in Cluny and its dependencies, it offered to the crusaders and pilgrims in the form of great sanctuaries along the trade and wander routes. A. Kingsley Porter first distinguished a chain of churches along the pilgrimage roads to Santiago as a homogeneous group: St. Martin in Tours, St. Foy in Conques (plate 47), St. Martial in Limoges, St. Sernin in Toulouse, and Santiago de Compostela.[75] They are a blend of Cluny III with the plans of St. Remi in Reims, St. Croix in Orléans and St. Maria im Kapitol in Cologne, combining aisled transepts and galleries. Sculptural decoration on their capitals and portals is very rich; the clear articulation of parts is similar to that of Cluny and Nevers. All were built between about 1060 and 1130.

A second group in this area worked with similar elements, but aimed for complication and colorful effects rather than clarity. Notre-Dame-du-Port in Clermont-Ferrand, St. Austremoine in Orcival (plates 84-86), and St. Paul in Issoire, all built in the early twelfth century, are representative of this type. Characteristically, the nave barrel vaults are left unarticulated by transverse arches. A single engaged shaft on either side of the nave, rising to the level of the gallery, creates a rhythmic accent without becoming an organizing factor. The crossing is flanked by pierced diaphragm arches on three sides and lit through windows in the wall over the apse. Narrow barrel-vaulted bays adjoining the crossing rise up high on either side of the crossing. Light from these bays enters the center indirectly through the pierced diaphragm arches, another detail of coloristic complication. The exterior features decorative patterns, polychrome masonry, and a rhythmic alternation of arched windows and shallow rectangular niches with inscribed colonnettes, all elements surviving from the *premier art roman* (for example, St. Généroux, tenth century).

In the Poitou the international provincial tradition is even more dominant. The characteristic "basilical hall" elevations combine a barrel-vaulted nave without clerestory with lower groin vaulted side aisles. St. Savin-sur-Gartempe (ca. 1060 f.), with round columns in the earlier portions of its nave and a barrel vault articulated only by the painted figures of its twelfth century fresco cycle, represents the earlier phase of the Poitou group. Notre-Dame-la-Grande in Poitiers, ca. 1100 f., (plates 81, 82) is rather more clearly articulated. The round barrel vault covering the nave is divided by transverse arches springing from compound piers, a square core with four engaged columns. Its façade, ordered by three tiers of blind arcades, is overspun by a tapestry-like profusion of sculpture in relief and three-quarter round. Two flanking towers, consisting of a column cluster topped by a circular arcade and "pine cone" spires, complete this eminently pictorial composition. The flanks of the building are sober by comparison. A blind arcade of massive buttresses gives plastic relief to the side walls.

The Périgord developed a distinct Romanesque type of single-naved hall churches. Massive piers along the interior walls carry domes on pendentives, forming a succession of domical bays. The interior of Angoulême Cathedral, begun ca. 1105 (plate 83), is exemplary. While accomplished by wholly different means, the result may be compared with parallel solutions at Speyer and Milan.

The resemblance of St. Front in Périgueux to S. Marco in Venice has been the cause of much discussion. But a domed building in the western Mediterranean such as S. Saturno in Cagliari on Sardinia (fifth century)[76] is not only geographically closer to the Aquitaine, but its massive ashlar masonry is a more likely point of departure for Périgord Romanesque than the mosaic and marble encrusted walls of S. Marco.

The increasing complication of Romanesque articulation in the twelfth century, subdividing space, walls, and membering into ever smaller units, had an inevitable result: the clarity achieved by the juxtaposition of large geometrical parts was lost in an overabundance of detail; surfaces and spaces merged into a reunified whole. This stylistic phenomenon mirrors a complex of twelfth-century social, political, and liturgical developments. The relatively simple socio-political categories of feudal society slowly gave way to the more complicated groupings of the waning Middle Ages. The new bourgeois class with its commercial wealth not only sought a greater share of political influence, but expressed its economic strength by greater participation in the building of the cathedrals which increasingly became symbols of the power of the cities. But financial contributions entitled the donors to privileges, especially the right of burial *ad sanctos,* either inside the churches or in adjoining mausolea-chapels. Since these chapels also contained reliquary altars, usually dedicated to the donor's patron saint, they were subordinate martyria in the sense we have discussed. If the articulation of medieval churches reflects their character as "compound martyria," the multiplication of such additions would require not only larger buildings, but increased subdivision of the available space. The culmination of this development were churches completely surrounded by chapels within a unified framework, such as Notre-Dame of Paris after about 1235.[77]

The degree of social, political, and economic evolution differed in the various parts of twelfth-century Europe, contributing to the solidification of regional and national linguistic and cultural patterns. The contrast between "Late Romanesque" architecture in the Holy Roman Empire and "Early Gothic" in northern France is based on valid stylistic distinctions. On the other hand, these different trends are parallel and logical developments of the various Romanesque solutions in their respective regions, arriving by different means at distinct, but not wholly unrelated ends.

Speyer II was the highpoint of Romanesque architecture in the Empire. Later buildings echoed this prototype, but with increasing complications of form and color, recalling Ottonian solutions. The Cathedrals at Mainz and Worms (plates 94, 95) were major projects which extended into the thirteenth century. In the western choirs of both, dwarf galleries, deeply incised blind arcades and colonnette bundles penetrate the masonry masses in rhythmic clusters. The impressive grouping of towers around the choir of the Tournai Cathedral[78] (late twelfth century and after) and the superimposition of arcaded tiers in the nave (plates 96, 97) indicate the same trend toward increasing size and complexity by multiplication of traditional elements of mass and articulation.

With the introduction of ribbed groin vaults at the Durham Cathedral[79] (plates 77-80) over an elevation very like that of Jumièges (plates 55-57), the Norman system was extended to all dimensions of the building. This Norman tradition, with its emphasis on wall penetration and the reduction of masonry masses to the functioning structural membering, was the essential prelude to later developments on the continent. Various elements at Durham tend toward spatial unification. The decorative patterns of the piers lead the eye past the barriers dividing nave and aisles, while the round *torus* profile of the vault ribs is much less of a block to visual transitions from part to part than the sharply definitive rectangular outline of contemporary Lombard ribs. Two rectangular rib vaults over each square bay of the alternating system complicate the simple succession of spaces as established at Speyer and in the choir of the Trinity in Caen. In addition the diagonal arches of the vaults are "depressed," so that the crown of the vaults is no higher than the apex of the transverse arches. The distinction of separate bays with domical vaults as at S. Ambrogio or Angoulême is sharply diminished: the road to the Gothic is open.

The evolution from the Early Christian "martyrium group" to the medieval "compound martyrium" has run as a leading theme through our discussion. We return to it once more with two monuments marking this evolution in a curious contrast of medieval possibilities. At the twelfth-century complex in Bologna known as S. Stefano the whole range of buildings at the side of the Holy Sepulchre was reproduced in a famous medieval "Jerusalem."[80] The layout is much older, but the present structures (much restored) date from about 1150. Anastasis, Golgotha, and Martyrion face each other across an arcaded courtyard. A few characteristic elements of the original were selected and combined freely, as is usual in medieval "copies," but the source is unmistakable. At almost the same time the original complex at the Holy Sepulchre in Jerusalem itself—or what remained of it—was "medievalized."[81] The Anastasis rotunda, Golgotha, the Martyrion and all surrounding sites were enveloped within the fabric of the "Crusader's Church," dedicated in 1149. The martyrium group par excellence had become a compound martyrium.

41

1.(a) For example, the problems of 1) martyrium, "congregational hall" and their various forms and combinations; 2) continuous, multi-partite and "dwarf" transepts together with the related questions of triple apses and/or side chambers or alcoves (e.g., at Old St. Peter's) and their possible role in the elaborate Early Christian offertory cult; 3) central and longitudinal buildings of different types with or without towers and/or domes; 4) baptisteries and tombs as an aspect of the martyrium problem; 5) *sub divo* (open air) Christian cult sites; 6) atrium and narthex; 7) burial *ad sanctos*, catacombs, *ad corpus* basilicas, "basilica-cemeteries," circumambulation of tombs and holy sites and their possible importance for the development of crypt and ambulatory; 8) the role of the altar and its location near or over a holy site, martyr's tomb or deposit of relics; 9) palace chapels and the role of galleries in central buildings and basilicas; 10) the mass and its evolution since pre-Constantinian times; 11) orientation; 12) "church families," i.e., groups of churches with various possible functions at one site; 13) the role of processions in the ritual, perhaps as a reflection of the so-called "station" services in Rome, Jerusalem, and elsewhere; 14) the complexities of varying liturgies and rituals in various parts of the Early Christian world and the importance of the reforms of Gregory the Great (590–604) for the western development. See in particular, André Grabar, *Martyrium, Recherches sur le Culte des Reliques et l'Art Chrétien Antique*, Paris, 1946; cf. also R. Krautheimer, Review of Grabar, *Art Bulletin*, XXXV, 1953, pp. 57 f.

(b) *Transepts* — A recent review: R. Krautheimer, "Il transetto nella basilica paleocristiana," *Actes du Ve Congrès International d'Archéologie Chrétienne (Aix-en-Provence, 1954)*, Vatican City-Paris, 1957, pp. 283 f.

(c) *Cruciform churches* — A debatable but important thesis: S. Guyer, *Grundlagen mittelalterlicher abendländischer Baukunst*, Einsiedeln-Zürich, 1950.

(d) *Domes* — E. Baldwin Smith, *The Dome*, Princeton, 1950.

(e) *Baptisteries and tombs* — R. Krautheimer, "Introduction to an 'Iconography of Medieval Architecture,'" *Journal of the Warburg and Courtauld Institutes*, V, 1942, pp. 1 f.

(f) *Burial ad sanctos, "basilica-cemeteries" and ambulatories* — A. Grabar, *op.cit.*; R. Krautheimer, "Mensa — Coemeterium — Martyrium," *Cahiers Archéologiques*, XI, 1960, pp. 15 f.

(g) *Altars* — Basic introduction: J. Braun, *Der christliche Altar in seiner geschichtlichen Entwicklung*, Munich, 1924.

(h) *Liturgy, Ritual and the Mass* — Still basic: L. Duchesne, *Origines du culte chrétien. Étude sur la liturgie latine avant Charlemagne*, 5th ed., Paris, 1925. Cf. also G. Dix, *The Shape of the Liturgy*, 1945.

2. R. Krautheimer, "The Constantinian Basilica of the Lateran," *Antiquity*, XXXIV, 1960, pp. 201 f.

3. Cf. note 1b *supra*.

4. Cf. note 1f *supra*.

5. R. Krautheimer, "Sancta Maria Rotonda," in *Arte del primo millennio*, Turin, 1953, pp. 21 f.

6. For a review of recent literature concerning these buildings cf. H. E. Kubach, "Die vorromanische und romanische Baukunst in Mitteleuropa; Literaturbericht 1950–54 mit Nachträgen für die Jahre 1938–50," *Zeitschrift für Kunstgeschichte*, XVIII, 1955, pp. 157 f.; also reports in *Neue Ausgrabungen in Deutschland*, Berlin, 1958.

7. Trier: Th. K. Kempf, "Frühchristliche Funde und Forschungen in Deutschland, *Actes du Ve Congrès International d'Archéologie Chrétienne, 1954*, Vatican City-Paris, 1957, pp. 68 f.

8. Cf. P. de Palol Salellas, "Los monumentos paleocristianos y visigódos estudiados en España desde el año 1939 a 1954," *Actes du Ve Congrès International d'Archéologie Chrétienne, 1954*, Vatican City-Paris, 1957, pp. 87 f.

9. Cf. E. Hegel in *Werdendes Abendland an Rhein und Ruhr*, Villa Hügel-Essen, 1956, pp. 145 f. Also B. Bischoff and F. Masai in *Settimane di Studio del Centro Italiano di Studi sull'Alto Medioevo, IV, 1956*, Spoleto, 1957, pp. 121 ff.

10. E.g., H. Focillon, *L'An Mil*, Paris, 1952, and his *Art d'Occident*, Paris, 1938.

11. H. Pirenne, *Mohammed and Charlemagne*, Meridian Books edition, New York, 1957, pp. 17–144; cf. also R. Buchner in *Settimane di Studio... V, 1957*, Spoleto, 1958, pp. 223 ff.

12. R. Krautheimer, "An Oriental Basilica in Rome: S. Giovanni a Porta Latina," *American Journal of Archaeology*, XL, 1936, pp. 485 f.; idem, *Corpus Basilicarum Christianarum Romae*, Vatican City-New York, 1937 f., *passim*.

13. Cf. W. Boekelmann, "Grundformen im frühkarolingischen Kirchenbau des östlichen Frankenreiches," *Wallraf-Richartz Jahrbuch*, XVIII, 1956, pp. 27–69 (a useful, but not complete compendium of such buildings); also G. Webb, *Architecture in Britain, the Middle Ages*, Baltimore, 1956, pp. 4 f.

14. Beda Venerabilis *(Vita Quinque Sanctorum Abbatum*, J. Migne, *Patrologia latina*, XCIV, col. 713 f.) refers precisely to these Northumbrian churches as built "iuxta Romanorum.... morem." Contrary W. Boeckelmann, *loc. cit.*

15. J. Puig i Cadafalch, *Le premier art roman*, Paris, 1928; idem, *La géographie et les origines du premier art roman*, Paris, 1935.

16. J. Hubert, "Germigny-des-Près," *Congrès Archéologique*, XCIII (Orléans), 1930, p. 534; A. Khatchatrian, "Notes sur l'architecture de l'église de Germigny-des-Près," *Cahiers archéologiques*, VII, 1956, pp. 161 f.

17. O. Müller, *Die Einharts-Basilika zu Steinbach bei Michelstadt im Odenwald*, Seligenstadt, 1939. F. Behn, "Neue Ausgrabungen und Untersuchungen an der Einharts-Basilika zu Steinbach im Odenwald," *Mainzer Zeitschrift*, XXVI, 1932, pp. 1 f.

18. R. Krautheimer, "The Carolingian Revival of Early Christian Architecture," *Art Bulletin*, XXIV, 1942, pp. 1 f.; for a reconstruction of the fifth century cf. A. Frazer, *A Graphic Reconstruction of Old St. Peter's, ca. 423*, M. A. Dissertation (unpubl.), Institute of Fine Arts, New York University, 1957. Cf. also J. Toynbee and J. Ward Perkins, *The Shrine of St. Peter's and The Vatican Excavations*, New York, 1957, pp. 240 f.

19. W. Meyer-Barkhausen, "Die frühmittelalterlichen Vorbauten am Atrium von Alt-St. Peter in Rom, zweitürmige Atrien, Westwerke und karolingisch-ottonische Königskapellen," *Wallraf-Richartz Jahrbuch*, XX, 1958, pp. 7 f.

20. H. Halm, "Die Ausgrabungen am Fuldaer Domplatz im Jahre 1953," in *St. Bonifatius*, Fulda, 1954, pp. 641 f.; cf. also W. Meyer-Barkhausen, "Die Ausgrabungen auf dem Fuldaer Domplatz 1953 in Neuer Sicht," *Zeitschrift des Vereins für Hessische Geschichte und Landeskunde*, LXVII, 1956, pp. 23 f.

21. Cf. note 1 *supra* and cf. William MacDonald's volume in this series.

22. A martyrium may be in its original place or recreated in a different location by the transfer *(translatio)* of all or part of the relic or of objects which have touched the relic *(pignora* or *brandea)*. A martyrium could be a cave (Nativity Church, Bethlehem; St. Thecla, Meriamlik-Seleucia); a subterranean tomb chamber (St. Menas near Alexandria); a burial chamber, *arcosolium* or simple *loculus* in a catacomb cemetery below (S. Agnese, Rome), or in a hillside near ground level (S. Lorenzo, Rome); or an open air *(sub divo)* shrine (Salona-Marusinac; St. Peter's *memoria* in Rome; column of St. Symeon at Kalat Siman).

23. Church groups were common from the fourth century on, in various arrangements depending on the site involved. Formal groupings in the manner of Hellenistic-Roman sanctuaries and *fora* were frequent. The Forum of Trajan contains equivalents of most aspects of later church groups. (Cf. L. Crema, *L'archittettura romana* [*Enciclopedia classica*, Sez. III, Vol. XII, Tome I], Turin, 1959, pp. 358 f., fig. 153. Columns as funerary monuments: L. Crema, *ibid.*, pp. 504 f.). Individual units might lie parallel to each other, with two basilicas flanking a baptismal building between or next to them (Trier, Aquileia, Salona), or mark several sites around a martyrium in an open courtyard (Gerasa, Naples, Cimitile-Nola, Jerusalem). Sometimes the component buildings were scattered within the limits of a precinct without a strict geometrical relationship (St. Menas, St. Thecla), following the tradition of older Greek sanctuaries (Athens, Olympia).

23a. J. Toynbee and J. Ward Perkins, *op.cit.*, pp. 206 f. Cf. also R. Krautheimer, "Mensa ...," *passim.*

24. The various early solutions to this problem may be understood in this light. For example, the disposition of four basilical arms around the tomb of St. John in Ephesos allowed for the presence of numerous pilgrims near the martyrium and processional circumambulation of the site without interrupting the services at the tomb itself. A similar arrangement with galleries over the aisles of the sixth-century building in Salonica built around the subterranean reliquary chamber containing a phial with blood of St. Demetrios, increased the possibilities of approach to the relic while allowing for other possible liturgical demands, e.g., the separation of men and women. Vaulted passages under the semicircular steeped priests' benches *(synthrona)* arranged in the apses of numerous Eastern churches (e.g., St. John of the Studion in Constantinople, fifth century), may have served such processions. Ambulatories, either surrounding the solid wall of an apse (e.g., at Miletus), or an apse pierced by the openings of an arcade as in the fourth-century "basilica-cemeteries" in Rome are another solution to this exigency.

25. J. Toynbee and J. Ward Perkins, *op. cit.*; cf. also the official report: B. M. Apollony Ghetti, A. Ferrua, E. Josi, and E. Kirschbaum, *Esplorazioni sotto la confessione di San Pietro in Vaticano*, Vatican City, 1951.

26. O. Müller, "Die Einhartsbasilika zu Seligenstadt am Main," *Forschungen und Fortschritte*, 1937, pp. 373 f.; *idem*, "Instandsetzung der Basilika in Seligenstadt," *Deutsche Kunst und Denkmalpflege*, 1954, pp. 26 f.; cf. E. Lehmann, *Der frühe deutsche Kirchenbau*, Berlin, 1938, 2nd ed., 1949, p. 98.

27. Similar ideas have been expressed in recent studies by J. Hubert, E. Lehmann and P. Francastel: cf. H. E. Kubach, *Literaturbericht 1955*, p. 161; also S. Guyer, *op.cit.*, pp. 74–76: "Baugruppe" and "Gruppenbau"; and A. Schmidt, "Westwerke und Doppelchöre," *Westfälische Zeitschrift*, CVI, 1956, pp. 347 f.

28. This phenomenon is not wholly unprecedented. At the Holy Sepulchre, for example, several adjacent martyria were incidental to the site. Professor Grabar has applied the term "martyria collectifs" to structures enclosing the remains of more than one martyr and cited the cemetery chapel at Tipasa (North Africa) as an example. The multiplication of martyria at one site by translation of relics or *brandea* was apparently prompted by the desire for burial *ad sanctos*: the more important and/or numerous the relics, the better. By transferring the bodies of three Apostles to the Church of the Holy Apostles in Constantinople, the Emperor Constantinius provided a major early precedent for the subsequent encyclopedic accumulations of martyria within one architectural context. The Apostoleion was flanked by Constantine's mausoleum, containing cenotaphs (memorials without relics) of all twelve Apostles. The transformation of tombs *ad sanctos* into subsidiary martyria by post-mortem canonization, may be another factor contributing to growth of "compound martyria."

Apostoleion: Texts in A. Heisenberg, *Grabeskirche und Apostelkirche, zwei*

Basiliken Konstantins, II, Leipzig, 1908. A comprehensive study of the successive buildings on the site of the Holy Apostles is in progress at Dumbarton Oaks.

29. Cf. note 5 *supra*.

30. Cf. R. Krautheimer, "Carolingian Revival...," p. 36, n. 202.

31. G. B. Giovenale, *La Basilica di S. Maria in Cosmedin*, Rome, 1927, pp. 35 f.; 322 f., and plates.

32. *Rear crypts*; A. Verbeek, "Die Aussenkrypta," *Zeitschrift für Kunstgeschichte*, XIII, 1950, pp. 7 f. — *Annular and ambulatory crypts*: H. Claussen, "Spätkarolingische Umgangskrypten im sächsischen Gebiet," *Forschungen zur Kunstgeschichte und christlichen Archäologie. III. Karolingische und Ottonische Kunst*, Wiesbaden, 1957, pp. 118 f. (with further bibliography).

33. *Facsimile edition*: H. Reinhardt, *Der St. Galler Klosterplan*, St. Gallen, 1952, with critical commentary.

34. According to the ninth-century abbot Angilbert in F. Lot, *Hariulf, Chronique de l'abbaye de Saint-Riquier*, Paris, 1894, p. 61.

35. R. Krautheimer, *Art Bulletin*, XXXV, 1953, p. 61.

36. *S. Lorenzo in Lucina*: R. Krautheimer and W. Frankl, "Recent Discoveries in Roman Churches," *American Journal of Archaeology*, XLIII, 1939, pp. 388 f.
    Koja Kalessi (Alahan Monastir): P. Verzone, *Alahan Monastir, un monumento dell'arte tardo romano in Isauria*, Turin, 1955.
    S. Lorenzo, Milan: A. Calderini, G. Chierici, and C. Cecchelli, *La Basilica Maggiore di S. Lorenzo in Milano*, Milan, 1951. Cf. review by C. R. Morey and R. Krautheimer in *Art Bulletin*, XXXV, 1953, pp. 151 f.
    S. Vitale, Ravenna: D. Maioli, *Il tempio di San Vitale in Ravenna*, Faenza, 1903; F. W. Deichmann, *Frühchristliche Bauten und Mosaiken von Ravenna*, Baden-Baden, 1958.

37. "Baugulf built the eastern temple... Ratger the wise architect joined a western temple to the other of wonderful art and great size, making (them) into one church."
    St. Maurice d'Agaune: L. Blondel, *Saint-Maurice d'Agaune*, St. Maurice, 1951.
    Cologne: O. Doppelfeld, "Stand der Grabungen und Forschungen am Alten Dom von Köln," in *Forschungen zur Kunstgeschichte und christlichen Archäologie. 1. Neue Beiträge zur Kunstgeschichte des 1. Jahrtausend. 2. Frühmittelalterliche Kunst*, Baden-Baden, 1954, pp. 69–100.
    Fulda: G. von Bezold, "Zur Geschichte der romanischen Baukunst in der Erzdiözese Mainz," *Marburger Jahrbuch für Kunstwissenschaft*, VIII/IX, 1936, pp. 1 f. Cf. also R. Krautheimer, "Carolingian Revival," *Art Bulletin*, XXIV, 1942, p. 5, n. 35, and note 20 *supra*. *St. Denis*: While attempting to avoid illustrating this discussion with "problematic" buildings when other material is available, I would like to draw attention to the important work done at St. Denis, by Prof. Sumner McKnight Crosby, *The Abbey of St. Denis*, 475–1122, I, New Haven, 1942; *idem*, *L'abbaye royale de Saint-Denis*, Paris, 1953.

38. A good recent bibliography of westwork literature may be found in W. Zimmermann, H. Borger et al., *Die Kirchen zu Essen-Werden*, Essen, 1959, p. 154, n. 4. Cf. also p. 159, n. 143. — Still the best basic survey of the monuments and documents: H. Reinhardt and E. Fels, "Étude sur les églises porches carolingiennes et leurs survivances dans l'art roman," *Bulletin monumental*, XCII, 1933, pp. 335 f.; XCVI, 1937, pp. 425 f.

39. *Centula*: W. Effmann, *Centula-St. Riquier. Eine Untersuchung zur Geschichte der kirchlichen Baukunst der Karolingerzeit*, Münster, 1912, G. Durand, *L'Église de St. Riquier. La Picardie historique et monumentale*, IV, Amiens-Paris, 1907 f.; cf. also I. Achter, "Zur Rekonstruktion der karolingischen Klosterkirche Centula," *Zeitschrift für Kunstgeschichte*, XIX, 1956, pp. 133 f.
    Corvey: W. Effmann, *Die Kirche der Abtei Corvey*, ed. A. Fuchs, Paderborn, 1929; H. Thümmler, "Die karolingische Baukunst in Westfalen," in *Forschungen*

. . . III, *Karolingische und Ottonische Kunst*, Wiesbaden, 1957, pp. 84 f.; W. Rave, *Corvey*, Münster, 1958.

Werden: W. Zimmermann, H. Borger, *et al.*, *op.cit.* (cf. note 38 *supra*).

40. Cf. W. Zimmermann and H. Borger, *op.cit.*, pp. 48–51 and, particularly, pp. 85 f. As Borger suggests, the history of Werden is probably more complicated than the sources indicate. But even if the *aedificio turris* mentioned in a letter of 876–77 (*op.cit.* p. 85) is not the *turris sanctae Mariae* dedicated in 943, but the central part of a preceding three-tower façade as reconstructed by Zimmermann (*op.cit.*, pp. 22 f.), the documents do not specifically identify either this or the later westwork as the seat of the court or as parish church. They could refer to the church as a whole.

41. E. Stefany, "Der Dom zu Aachen," *Das Münster*, X, 1957, pp. 401 f. Cf. recently also F. Kreusch, "Ueber Pfalzkapelle und Atrium zur Zeit Karls des Grossen," in *Dom zu Aachen, Beiträge zur Baugeschichte IV*, Aachen, 1958; and W. Boeckelmann, "Von den Ursprüngen der Aachener Pfalzkapelle," *Wallraf-Richartz Jahrbuch*, XIX, 1957, pp. 9 f.

42. Cf. R. Krautheimer, "Carolingian Revival," pp. 34 f. —. H. Fichtenau (*Byzanz und die Pfalz zu Aachen*, Vienna, 1951) has focused on the *Chrysotriklinos*, the throne room of the long-destroyed Byzantine "Great Palace" while Grabar refers to the adjoining eighth-century chapel of the Virgin of the Pharos (*op.cit.*, I, pp. 565 f.). S. Lorenzo in Milan with its atrium and towers and S. Vitale — both possibly "palace chapels" — loom in the background.

43. P. Frankl, *Die frühmittelalterliche und romanische Baukunst (Handbuch der Kunstwissenschaft)*, Wildpark-Potsdam, 1926, p. 18.

44. Cf. P. Héliot, "Le chevet roman de Saint-Bertin à Saint-Omer et l'architecture franco-lotharingienne," *Revue Belge*, XXII, 1953, pp. 73 f.

45. L. Grodecki, *L'architecture Ottonnienne*, Paris, 1958, pp. 153 f.

46. H. T. Broadley, "A Reconstruction of the Tenth-Century Church of St. Cyriacus in Gernrode," *Marsyas*, New York, VI, 1950–53, pp. 25 f.

47. *Hagios Demetrios:* G. Soteriou, Ἡ βασιλικὴ τοῦ Ἁγίου Δημητρίου Θεσσαλονίκης, Athens, 1952.

    Bulgaria: B. Filov, *Geschichte der altbulgarischen Kunst*, Berlin-Leipzig, 1932. *Mesembria:* A. Rachenov, *Eglises de Mesembria*, Sofia, 1932; *Aboba-Pliska:* B. Filov, "Les Palais Vieux-Bulgares et les Palais Sassanides," in *L'Art Byzantin chez les Slaves. Les Balkans*, I, Paris 1930, pp. 80 f. fig. 6. Cf. *Aboba-Pliska*, *Isvestija Russk. Arch. Instituta v Konstantinopole*, Sofia, 1905.

48. J. Ebersolt and A. Thiers, *Les églises de Constantinople*, Paris, 1913, pp. 139 f., pls. 32–33; J. Ebersolt, *Monuments d'Architecture Byzantine*, Paris 1934, p. 57.

48a. H. Beseler and H. Roggenkamp, *Die Michaelis-Kirche in Hildesheim*, Berlin, 1954. Also O. Karpa, *Deutsche Kunst und Denkmalpflege*, 1960, pp. 57 f.

49. Cf. the literature cited by H. E. Kubach, *Literaturbericht 1955*, pp. 179 f., and L. Grodecki, *op.cit.*, *passim*.

50. G. Lanfry, "L'église carolingienne de Saint-Pierre de Jumièges," *Bulletin monumental*, XCVIII, 1939, pp. 47 f.

51. L. Grodecki, *op.cit.*, pp. 109 f. Documents: G. von Bezold, *op.cit.*, pp. 57 f., (cf. note 37 *supra*). While recent observers have tended to accept a double tower façade, H. Reinhardt's suggestion of a westwork is still worth serious consideration ("Das erste Münster zu Schaffhausen und die Frage der Doppelturmfassade am Mittelrhein," *Anzeiger für schweizerische Altertumskunde*, 1935, pp. 239 f.). Recent literature: H. E. Kubach, *Literaturbericht 1955*, p. 185.

52. H. Focillon, *L'An Mil*, Paris, 1952.

53. W. Meyer-Schwartau, *Der Dom zu Speyer*, Berlin, 1893. Still basic for Speyer chronology: R. Kautsch, "Der Dom zu Speyer," *Städel Jahrbuch*, I, 1921, pp. 75–108; a recent review of the Speyer literature: H. E. Kubach, "Miszellen zur

Baugeschichte des Speyerer Domes," *Zeitschrift für Kunstgeschichte*, XXII, 1959, pp. 353 f.

54. G. Lanfry, "Fouilles et découvertes à Jumièges," *Bulletin monumental*, LXXXVII, 1928, pp. 107 f.

55. E. Gall, *Niederrheinische und normannische Architektur im Zeitalter der Früh-gotik*. I., Berlin, 1915; *idem, Die Gotische Baukunst in Frankreich und Deutschland*. I. Leipzig, 1925; cf. also J. Bony, "La technique normande du mur épais à l'époque romane," *Bulletin monumental*, XCVIII, 1939, pp. 153 f.

56. E. Gall, *op.cit.*, 1925, pp. 17 and 110; L. Grodecki, *op.cit.*, pp. 191, 235, n. 35 with bibliography.

57. For example, in Nimes, the so-called "Temple of Diana," a Trajanic nympheum. (L. Crema, *L'architettura romana*, Turin, 1959, p. 466, figs. 540–41).

58. *St. Peter in Mistail*: E. Poeschel, *Die Kunstdenkmäler des Kantons Graubünden*, Basel, 1943.
S. Cristina de Lena: S. Frischauer, *Altspanischer Kirchenbau*, Berlin, 1930, pp. 71 f.; V. Lamperez y Romea, *Historia de la arquitectura cristiana española en la edad media*, Madrid, 1908–09, I, pp. 300 f.
Agliate: A. K. Porter, *Lombard Architecture*, New Haven, 1917, II, pp. 31 f.; but cf. also L. Grodecki, *op.cit.*, p. 148, n. 44.

59. J. Evans, *The Romanesque Architecture of the Order of Cluny*, Cambridge, 1938; *idem, Cluniac Art of the Romanesque Period*, Cambridge, 1950; K. J. Conant, *Carolingian and Romanesque Architecture 800 to 1200*, Baltimore, 1959, pp. 107 f.

60. J. Vallery-Radot, *Saint-Philibert de Tournus*, Paris, 1955.

61. Cf. H. Pirenne, *History of Europe*, I, Anchor edition, New York, 1958, pp. 248 f.

62. Common since Viollet-le-Duc's work *(Dictionnaire raisonné de l'architecture française du XIe au XVIe siècle*, Paris 1858–68), the conception of medieval architecture in terms of its *parts* (piers, buttresses, capitals, decoration, vaults, towers, ambulatories, etc.), each living out a kind of organic evolution of its own, has become inadequate. The *typological approach* of the German school (as represented in G. Dehio and G. v. Bezold, *Die kirchliche Baukunst des Abendlandes*, Stuttgart, 1884–1901), although still basic, is also often inconclusive, since various plan types of diverse origin may coexist within a region to which *other* elements give a stylistic unity. The architecture of Lombardy around 1100 is an example. Study of *structural features* as an index of "achievement" within the framework of an assumed technological development has likewise proven misleading, as shown by A. K. Porter, *(Medieval Architecture: Its origins and development*, New York, 1909, and his *Lombard Architecture*, New Haven, 1917). With his overriding interest in rib vaulting, Porter focuses on "Lombard" and "Norman" architecture and the earlier periods to the exclusion of all other Romanesque phenomena. With our present limited knowledge of medieval architectural theory and practice, the "function" or "adequacy" of given structural elements may be hard to determine, perhaps even wholly irrelevant. For the same reason the search for the origins of "motifs," for cultural and technical "priority," for *première* performances, has lost its impetus. Such factors remain secondary in an evaluation of Romanesque architecture. As Frankl *(op.cit.*, pp. 139 ff.) insisted nearly forty years ago, the building as a *structural and stylistic whole*, not the parts, is what matters. It is now also more generally admitted that an analysis based on regional "schools" (as, for example, most developed, if not most extended in R. de Lasteyrie, *L'Architecture religieuse en France à l'époque romane*, Paris, 1912), no matter how many may be distinguished or by what criteria they may be defined, has restricted validity in studying an art that is continental rather than sectional or national in scope. Similar spatial subdivision, achieved by domical groin vaults in the Rhineland and by diaphragm arches without vaults in Tuscany, relates the superficially different buildings of these two regions. Wholly divergent formal treatment of an apparently identical element,

such as rib vaults, on the other hand, distinguishes Anglo-Norman from Lombard architecture around 1100.

63. W. Horn, "Romanesque Churches in Florence and their Chronology and Stylistic Development," *Art Bulletin*, XXV, 1943, pp. 112 f. — The author's own observations at S. Miniato (uniform masonry along the entire lower part of the building) suggest that the present church was built wholly after about 1070.

64. Cf. R. Krautheimer's similar observations at Bari, "San Nicola in Bari und die apulische Architektur des 12. Jahrhunderts," *Wiener Jahrbuch für Kunstgeschichte*, IX, 1934, p. 16.

65. Cf. the author's article: "Early Renaissance Architectural Theory and Practice in Antonio Filarete's 'Trattato di Architettura,'" *Art Bulletin*, XLI, 1959, pp. 89 f. For tendencies in graphic representation, cf. H. Bober, "In Principio: Creation Before Time," *De Artibus Opuscula XL: Essays in Honor of Erwin Panofsky*, 1961.

66. Cf. note 53 *supra*.

67. *Xhignesse, Hamoir:* H. E. Kubach, *Zeitschrift für Kunstwissenschaft*, VII, 1953, pp. 120 f. and figs. *Hersfeld:* D. Groszmann, *Die Abteikirche zu Hersfeld*, Kassel, 1955; but cf. also W. Meyer-Barkhausen, "Zum Problem der Hersfelder Stiftsruine," *Wallraf-Richartz Jahrbuch*, XIX, 1957, pp. 264 f.

68. *S. Fedele in Como:* A. K. Porter, *Lombard Architecture*, II, New Haven, 1916, pp. 322 f. pls. 61 f.

69. H. Rahtgens, *Die Kirche St. Maria im Kapitol zu Köln*, Düsseldorf, 1913; cf. also H. E. Kubach, *Literaturbericht 1955*, p. 181.

70. E. Kluckhohn, "Gestalt und Geschichte der Ambrosiuskirche in Mailand," *Mitteilungen des kunsthistorischen Institutes in Florenz*, VI, 1940, pp. 73 f.

71. *Modena:* Cf. E. Kluckhohn, *op.cit.*, p. 93, with additional literature.

72. Cf. L. Grodecki, *op.cit.*, p. 93 f.; H. E. Kubach, *Literaturbericht 1955*, p. 191.

73. H. Thümmler, "Die Baukunst des 11. Jahrhunderts in Italien," *Römisches Jahrbuch für Kunstgeschichte*, III, 1939, pp. 210 f.; A. Pantoni, "Problemi Archeologici Cassinensi. La Basilica pre-Desideriana," *Rivista di Archeologia Cristiana*, XVI, 1939, pp. 271 f.; also Conant's restoration pl. VIIIA, in *Carolingian and Romanesque Architecture*, Baltimore, 1959.

73a. R. Krautheimer, *op. cit.*, note 64 *supra*.

74. F. Salet, *La Madeleine de Vézelay*, Melun, 1948.

75. A. K. Porter, *Romanesque Sculpture of the Pilgrimage Roads*, Boston, 1923; cf. K. J. Conant, *op.cit.*, pp. 91 f.

76. R. Delogu, *L'architettura del medioevo in Sardegna*, Rome, 1953, pp. 7 f.

77. M. Aubert, *Notre Dame de Paris*, Paris, 1920, pp. 34 f. — For the concept of "spatial unification" in Gothic architecture, cf. P. Frankl, "Der Beginn der Gotik und das allgemeine Problem des Stilbeginns," in *Festschrift Heinrich Wölfflin*, Munich, 1924.

78. A recent survey of the Tournai literature: P. Héliot, "Les parties romanes de la cathédrale de Tournay," *Revue Belge*, XXV, 1956, pp. 3 f.

79. J. Bilson, "Durham Cathedral and the chronology of its vaults," *Archeological Journal*, LXXIX, 1922, pp. 101 f.; G. Webb, *op.cit.*, p. 35.

80. R. Krautheimer, *op.cit.*, note 1e *supra*, pp. 17 f.

81. L. Vincent and F. Abel, *Jérusalem Nouvelle*, II, 1, Paris, 1914, pp. 89 f. — Plan: K. J. Conant, *op.cit.*, p. 208, fig. 52.

1. Old St. Peter's, Rome, 320 f. Plan (modified after Alfarano).

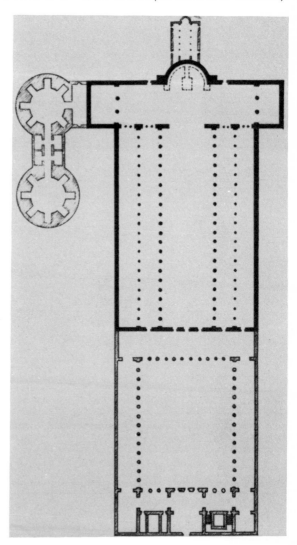

2. Escomb, Church, ca. 700.

3. Escomb, Church. Plan and elevation.

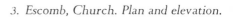

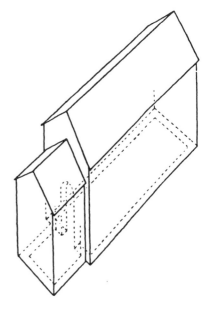

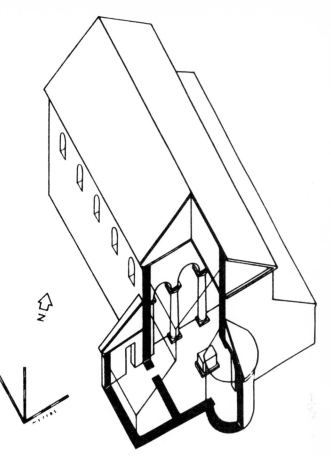

4. *St. Martin, Angers. Isometric projection.*

5. *S. Cristina de Lena, Asturia, early tenth century.*

6. *S. Cristina de Lena. Section.*

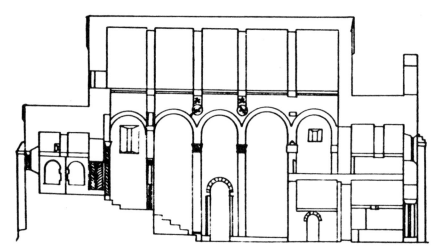

7. *S. Cristina de Lena. Interior.*

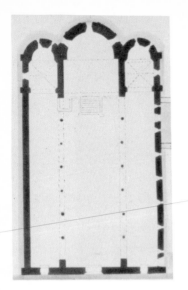

8. S. Piètro, Agliate, early eleventh century (?). Plan.

9. S. Pietro. Interior.

10. St. Lazare, Autun, ca. 1120–25. Nave.

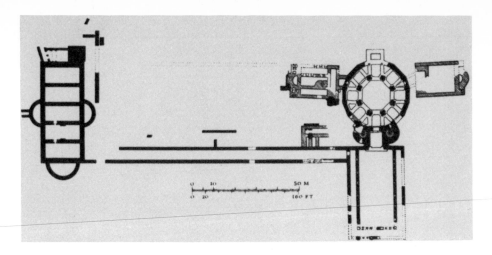

11. The Palace and Palatine Chapel, Aachen, late eighth–early ninth centuries. Plan.

12. Palatine Chapel. Reconstruction and plan.

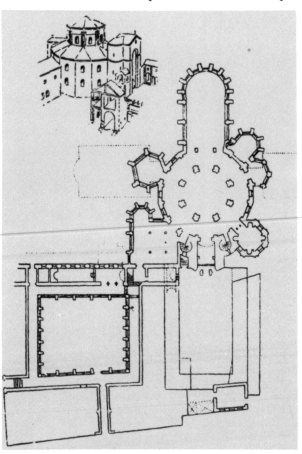

13. Palatine Chapel. Interior.

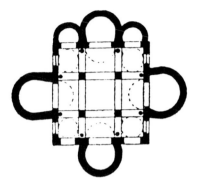

15. Germigny-des-Prés, 799–818. Plan.

16. Germigny-des-Prés. Watercolor by Delton, 1841.

17. *St. Riquier, Centula (Picardy), consecrated 799. Pétau engraving, 1612, after an eleventh-century manuscript illustration.*

18. *SS. Salvator and Bonifatius, Fulda, Carolingian Church and Atrium, 791–819. Plan.*

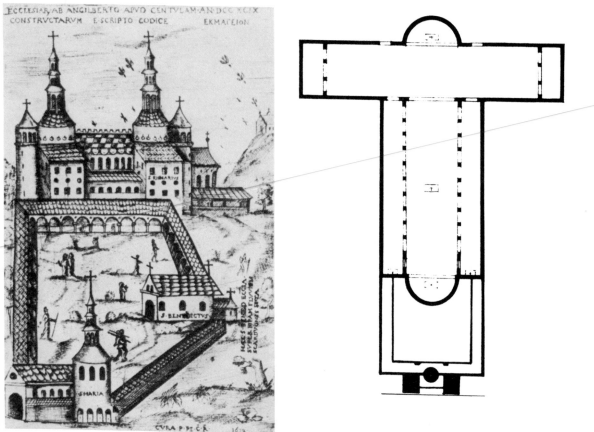

19. *St. Nazarius, Torhalle, Lorsch, late eighth century.*

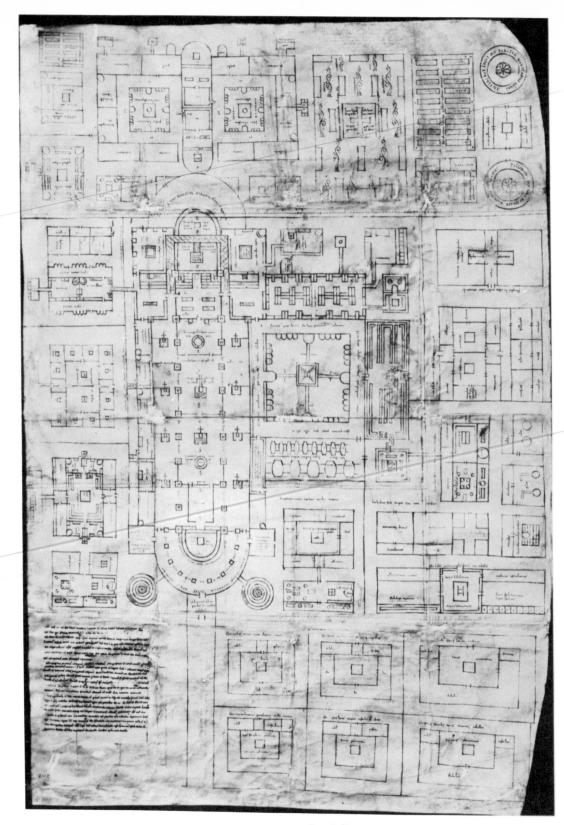

20. St. Gall, Monastery, early ninth century. Plan.

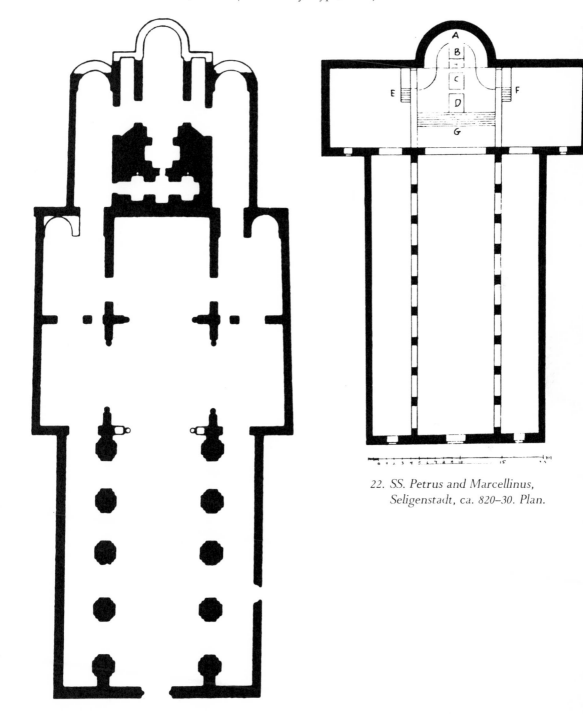

21. St. Philibert-de-Grandlieu, 814–19. (Ambulatory crypt, 836 f.). Plan.

22. SS. Petrus and Marcellinus, Seligenstadt, ca. 820–30. Plan.

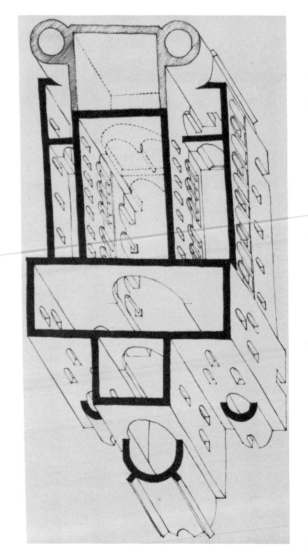

23. St. Cyriacus, Gernrode, tenth century. Isometric section modified.

24. *St. Cyriacus. Nave.*

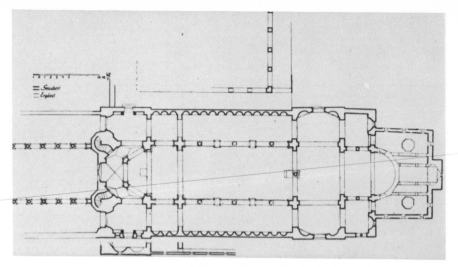

25. Münster, Essen, first half eleventh century. Plan.

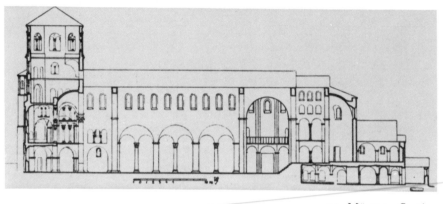

26. Münster. Section.

27. Münster. Exterior reconstruction.

28. Münster. Interior.

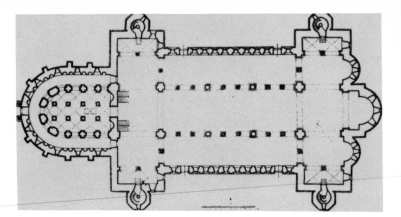

29. St. Michael, Hildesheim, ca. 1000–33. Plan.

30. St. Michael. Interior.

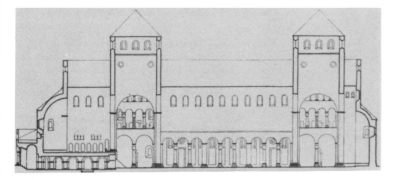

31. St. Michael. Reconstruction.

32. St. Michael. Interior, before 1033. Columns with cubic capitals.

33. *Abbey Church, Corvey, Saxony, 822 f. Westwork, groundfloor, interior, ca. 875.*

34. Abbey Church, Corvey. Westwork interior, ca. 875, after partial reconstruction.

35. Abbey Church, Corvey. Plan.

36. Abbey Church, Corvey. Westwork elevation.

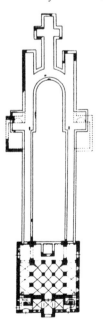

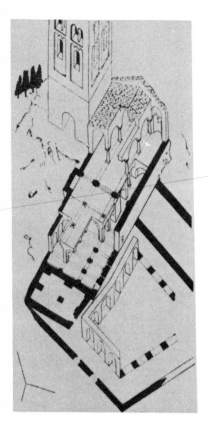

37. *St. Martin du Canigou (Pyrenees), 1001–26. Isometric section.*

38. *St. Martin. Interior, before reconstruction.*

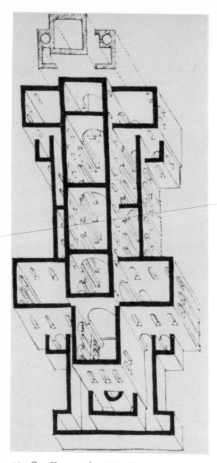

40. *St. Gertrude, Nivelles (Meuse) 1000–46. Isometric
perspective drawing modified after Grodecki.*

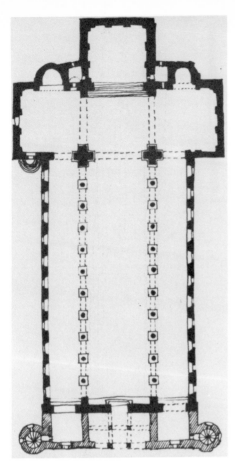

41. *Limburg on the Hardt, (Palatinate).*
Abbey, 1025 f. Plan.

42. *Limburg on the Hardt. Choir and crypt.*

43. *Limburg on the Hardt. Air view of transept.*

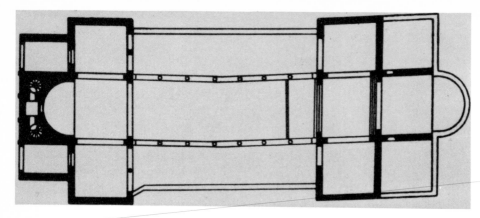

44. S. Maria, Mittelzell (Reichenau), 991–96 f. Plan.

45. S. Maria. Nave.

46. S. Maria. West tower, 1030–48.

47. *St. Foy, Conques, end of eleventh century. Interior.*

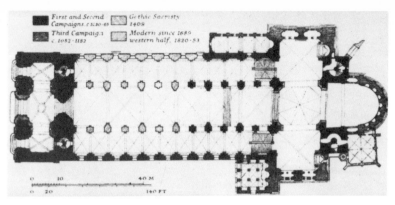

First and Second
Campaigns. c. 1030-65

Third Campaign.
c. 1082-1182

Gothic Sacristy
1408

Modern since 1689
western half, 1820-53

0 10 40 M
0 20 140 FT

48. *Speyer. Cathedral I, ca. 1030–60; Cathedral II, ca. 1080–1150. Plan.*

49. *Speyer. Cathedral II. Interior in the early nineteenth century. State after 1080–1105.*

50. Speyer. Cathedral II. Apse, state after 1080–1100.

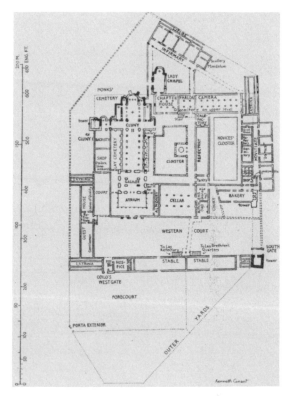

51. Cluny II and the Monastery as of ca. 1043. Plan.

*52. Cluny II and the Monastery.
Reconstruction drawing.*

53. Cluny III, 1088–1225. Reconstruction model.

54. *St. Etienne, Vignory, first half of the eleventh century. Nave.*

55. *Notre Dame, Jumièges, ca. 1040 f. View of interior from crossing.*

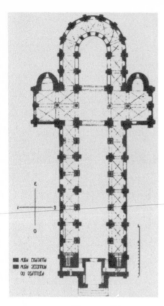

56. Notre Dame. Plan.

57. Notre Dame, Jumièges. Façade.

58. *S. Maria, Ripoll (Catalonia), nave, late tenth century, transept, 1018–32. View of exterior after reconstruction.*

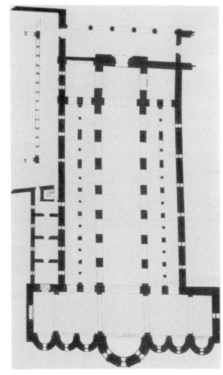

59. *S. Maria. Plan.*

60. *Paray-le-Monial (Saône et Loire). Abbey constructed early twelfth century.*

62. Paray-le-Monial. View of crossing.

63. *Montecassino, Abbey, ca. 1075 f. Plan of Antonio da Sangallo (sixteenth century).*

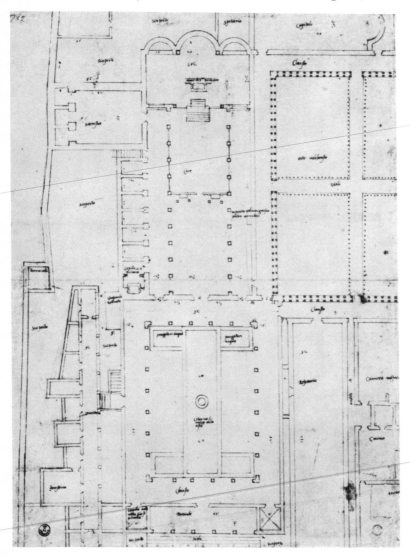

64. *Salerno, Cathedral, ca. 1077. Interior of transept.*

65. *S. Nicola, Bari, 1089 f. Exterior.*

66. *S. Nicola. Plan.*

67. *S. Nicola. Interior.*

68. *Trani (Apulia)*, Cathedral, 1097 f.

69. *St. Etienne, Caen. Façade, last third of eleventh century. (Upper part of towers later.)*

70. *Mont-Saint-Michel, Abbey, ca. 1060. South wall of nave.*

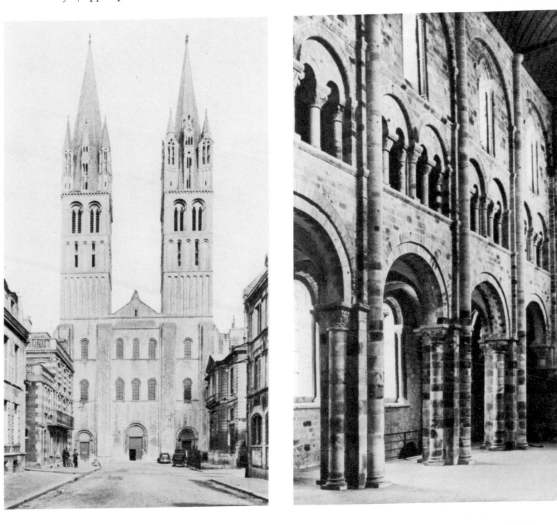

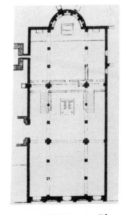

73. S. Miniato al Monte. Plan.

74. *Modena, Cathedral, early twelfth century. Interior. (The vaults are later.)*

75. *Modena, Cathedral. Exterior, early twelfth century and later.*

76. *S. Abbondio, Como, dedicated 1095.*

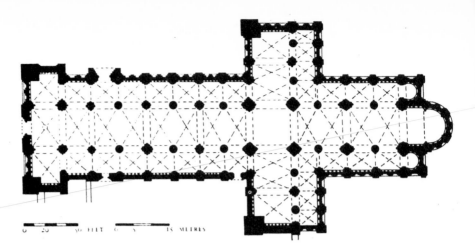

77. *Durham, Cathedral, early twelfth century. Plan.*

78. *Durham. Choir triforium.*

79. *Durham. Nave.*

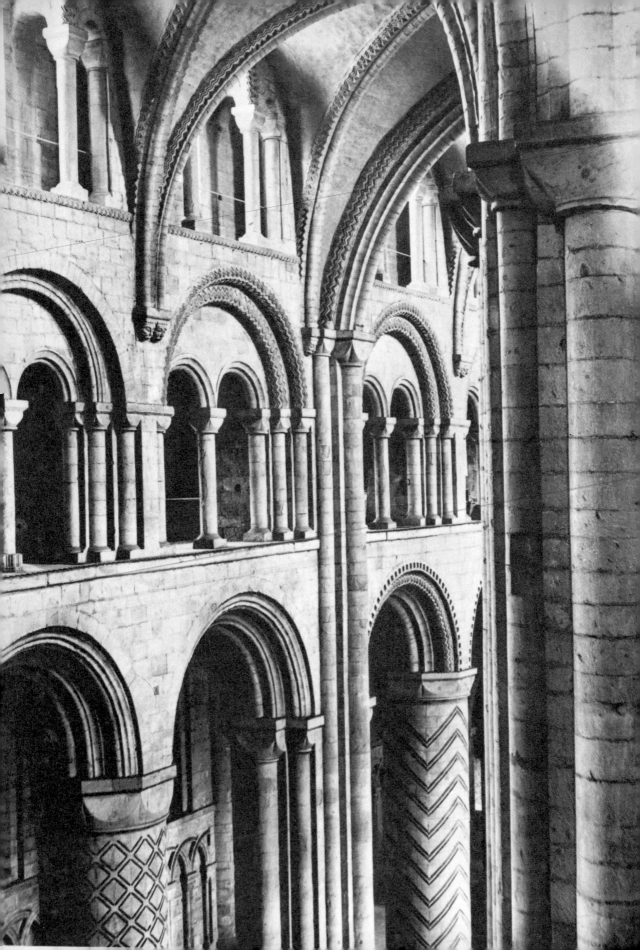

80. Durham. Interior cross view of transept triforium.

81. Notre-Dame-la-Grande, Poitiers (Vienne), first half of twelfth century.

82. Notre-Dame-la-Grande. Nave.

83. *Angoulême, Cathedral, early twelfth century. Nave.*

84. *St. Austremoine, Orcival, early twelfth century. Interior.*

85. *St. Austremoine.*
Section of transept.

87. *St. Etienne, Nevers, 1063–97. Interior.*

88. *St. Etienne. Plan.*

88. *St. Etienne. Plan.*

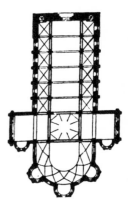

89. *St. Etienne. Exterior of apse. (Tower was originally higher.)*

91. *St. Madeleine. Porch with tympanum.*

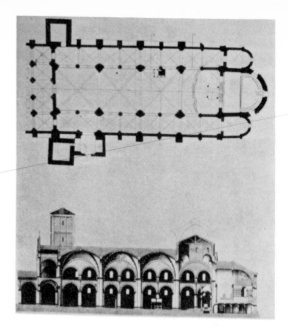

92. S. Ambrogio, Milan, late eleventh–early twelfth centuries. Plan and Section.

93. S. Ambrogio. Interior.

94. *Mainz, Cathedral. Western apse, end of twelfth century–thirteenth century.*

95. *Worms, Cathedral. Western apse, early thirteenth century.*

96. *Tournai, Cathedral. Nave, ca. 1150. Eastern end, later twelfth–thirteenth centuries.*

97. *Tournai. Exterior.*

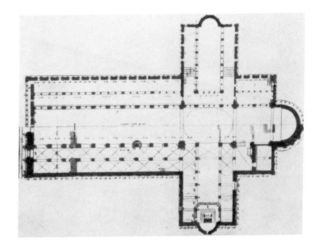

98. *S. Maria Maggiore, Pisa, 1063–twelfth century. Plan.*

99. *S. Maria Maggiore. Exterior.*

100. S. Maria Maggiore. Interior.

BIBLIOGRAPHY

The following works are listed in chronological order of publication within each section.

GENERAL

DEHIO, G. and BEZOLD, G. VON, *Die kirchliche Baukunst des Abendlandes*, Stuttgart, 1884–1901. – Still a basic *corpus* of medieval monuments.

LETHABY, W. R., *Medieval Art from the Peace of the Church to the Eve of the Renaissance*, rev. ed. by D. Talbot Rice, London, 1949 (orig. publ. 1904). –A traditional architect's view.

PORTER, A. KINGSLEY, *Medieval Architecture: Its Origins and Development*, New York, 1909.–An important statement, now outdated both in content and viewpoint: Romanesque architecture as a steppingstone on the road to the Gothic.

FRANKL, P., *Die frühmittelalterliche und romanische Baukunst*, Wildpark-Potsdam, 1926 (Handbuch der Kunstwissenschaft).–Now somewhat dated in content, this book is still important for its comprehensive approach, combining stylistic with structural considerations and for its emphasis on "Romanesque" as an independent style.

CLAPHAM, A. W., *Romanesque Architecture in Western Europe*, Oxford, 1936.–A useful brief survey in the tradition of Lethaby and Porter, emphasizing the importance of pre-Norman architecture in England.

FOCILLON, H., *Art d'Occident. Le Moyen-âge roman et gothique*, Paris, 1938. –A comprehensive view distinguishing northern from southern traditions.

BALTRUSAITIS, J., *L'église cloisonnée en Orient et Occident*, Paris 1941.

BRÉHIER, L., *Le style roman*, Paris, 1941.

MOREY, C. R., *Medieval Art*, New York, 1942.

FOCILLON, H., *Moyen-âge: Survivances et Réveils*, New York, 1943.

REY, R., *L'art roman et ses origines: archéologie pré-romane et romane*, Toulouse-Paris, 1945.

WEISBACH, W., *Religiöse Reform und mittelalterliche Kunst*, Einsiedeln-Zürich, 1945.

GUYER, S., *Grundlagen mittelalterlicher abendländischer Baukunst*, Einsiedeln-Zürich, 1950.–A debatable, but important thesis.

KUBACH, H. E., and VERBEEK, A., "Die vorromanische und romanische Baukunst in Mitteleuropa, Literaturbericht 1938–50," *Zeitschrift für Kunstgeschichte*, XIV, 1951, pp. 124 ff.

FOCILLON, H., *L'An Mil*, Paris, 1952.

KUBACH, H. E., "Die vorromanische und romanische Baukunst in Mitteleuropa," Literaturbericht 1950–54 mit Nachträgen für die Jahre 1938–50," *Zeitschrift für Kunstgeschichte*, XVIII, 1955, pp. 157 ff.

CONANT, K. J., *Carolingian and Romanesque Architecture: 800–1200*, Baltimore, 1959 (Pelican History of Art).

LITURGY AND ICONOGRAPHY

HAUCK, A., *Kirchengeschichte Deutschlands*, Leipzig, 1904.

DUCHESNE, L., *Origines du culte chrétien. Étude sur la liturgie latine avant Charlemagne*, 5th ed., Paris, 1925.–Still basic.

KRAUTHEIMER, R., "An Introduction to an 'Iconography of Mediaeval Architecture,'" *Journal of the Warburg and Courtauld Institutes*, V, 1942, pp. 1–33.

BANDMANN, G., *Mittelalterliche Architektur als Bedeutungsträger*, Berlin, 1951. – Broad in scope, but not always convincing in its conclusions.

KRAUTHEIMER, R., "Sancta Maria Rotonda," *Arte del primo millennio*, Turin, 1953, pp. 21 f. – Both of this author's studies are valued especially for their meticulous documentation and methodology.

SOURCES

SCHLOSSER, J. VON, *Schriftquellen zur Geschichte der karolingischen Kunst*, Vienna, 1896.

SCHLOSSER, J. VON, *Quellenbuch zur Kunstgeschichte des abendländischen Mittelalters*, Vienna, 1896.

MORTET, V., *Recueil de textes relatifs à l'histoire de l'architecture et la condition des architectes en France au moyen-âge*, Paris, 1911.

LEHMANN-BROCKHAUS, O., *Schriftquellen zur Kunstgeschichte des 11. und 12. Jahrhunderts für Deutschland, Lothringen und Italien*, Berlin, 1938.

PANOFSKY, E., *Abbot Suger on the Abbey Church of St.-Denis and its Art Treasures*, Princeton, 1946.

HOLT, E. G., *Literary Sources of Art History*, Princeton, 1947.

LEHMANN-BROCKHAUS, O., *Schriftquellen zur Kunst in England, Wales und Schottland vom Jahre 901 bis zum Jahre 1307*, Munich, 1955 f.

SCHLOSSER, J. VON, *La Letteratura artistica*, 2nd ed., rev. by Otto Kurz, trans. by Filippo Rossi, Vienna-Florence, 1956.

EARLY MEDIEVAL ARCHITECTURE

HUBERT, J., *L'art pré-roman*, Paris, 1938.

VERZONE, P., *L'architettura religiosa dell'alto medio evo nell'Italia settentrionale*, Milan, 1942.

HUBERT, J., *L'architecture religieuse du haut moyen-âge en France*, Paris, 1952.

FORSYTH, G., *The Church of St. Martin at Angers*, Princeton, 1953. – A specialized monograph with comments and literature ranging over the entire field of Early Medieval architecture.

Arte del primo millennio. Atti del II° convegno per lo studio dell'arte dell'alto medio evo tenuto presso l'università di Pavia nel Settembre 1950, Turin, 1953.

Atti del 2° Congresso Internazionale di Studi sull'Alto Medioevo, Sett. 1952, Spoleto, 1953.

Forschungen zur Kunstgeschichte und christlichen Archäologie. I. Neue Beiträge zur Kunstgeschichte des 1. Jahrtausend. Baden-Baden, 1952–54.

Frühmittelalterliche Kunst in den Alpenländern. Actes du IIIe Congrès International pour l'Étude du Haut Moyen-Age, 9–14 Septembre, 1951), Lausanne, 1954.

Settimane di Studio del Centro Italiano di Studi sull'Alto Medioevo, Spoleto, 1954. – A continuing series of scholarly contributions, each volume centering on an important theme of early medieval culture.

CAROLINGIAN ARCHITECTURE

CLEMEN, P., *Die romanische Monumentalmalerei in den Rheinlanden*, Düsseldorf, 1916. – Basic for study of Aix-la-Chapelle.

MEYER-BARKHAUSEN, W., "Karolingische Kapitelle in Hersfeld, Höchst a. M. und Fulda," *Zeitschrift für bildende Kunst*, LXIII, 1929–30, pp. 126 ff.

GALL, E., *Karolingische und Ottonische Kirchen*, Burg bei Magdeburg, 1930.

HINKS, R., *Carolingian Art*, London, 1935.

LEHMANN, EDG., *Der frühe deutsche Kirchenbau*, Berlin, 1938, 2nd ed., 1949.

KRAUTHEIMER, R., "The Carolingian Revival of Early Christian Architecture," *Art Bulletin*, XXIV, 1942, pp. 1 ff. – An important contribution to our understanding of Carolingian architecture.

BOECKELMANN, W., "Grundformen im frühkarolingischen Kirchenbau des östlichen Frankenreiches," *Wallraf-Richartz Jahrbuch*, XVIII, 1956, pp. 27 ff.

GALL, E., *Dome und Klosterkirchen am Rhein*, Munich, 1956.

Forschungen zur Kunstgeschichte und christlichen Archäologie. III. *Karolingische und Ottonische Kunst*, Wiesbaden, 1957. – Important recent studies and excavations.

OTTONIAN ARCHITECTURE

RAVE, P. O., *Der Emporenbau in romanischer und frühgotischer Zeit*, Bonn-Leipzig, 1924.

BEENKEN, H., "Die ausgeschiedene Vierung," *Repertorium für Kunstwissenschaft*, X, 1930, pp. 207. – An important statement on a basic problem in the development of medieval architecture.

LICHT, E., *Ottonische und frühromanische Kapitelle in Deutschland*, Diss. Marburg, 1934. – A useful survey.

JANTZEN, H., *Ottonische Kunst*, Munich, 1947 (ed. Rowohlt-Hamburg, 1959). – A good introduction to the subject.

KUBACH, H. E., "Die frühromanische Baukunst des Maaslandes," *Zeitschrift für Kunstwissenschaft*, VII, 1953, pp. 113. – A survey of lesser known but well preserved Ottonian buildings in Belgium.

BESELER, H. and ROGGENKAMP, H., *Die Michaeliskirche in Hildesheim*, Berlin, 1954.

SWARZENSKI, H., *Monuments of Romanesque Art. The Art of Church Treasures in North Western Europe*, Chicago-London, 1955.

ZIMMERMANN, W., *Das Münster zu Essen*, Essen, 1956.

GALL, E., *Dome und Klosterkirchen am Rhein*, Munich, 1956.

Forschungen zur Kunstgeschichte und christlichen Archäologie. III. *Karolingische und Ottonische Kunst*, Wiesbaden, 1957.

ZIMMERMANN, W., BORGER, H., et al., *Die Kirchen zu Essen-Werden*, Essen, 1959.

GRODECKI, L., *L'architecture ottonienne*, Paris, 1958. – A broad synthetic view with literature up to date of publication.

INTERNATIONAL PROVINCIAL ARCHITECTURE SIXTH TO ELEVENTH CENTURIES

RIVOIRA, G. T., *Lombardic Architecture: its Origin, Development and Derivatives*, trans. by G. Mc. N. Rushforth, Oxford, 1910, 2nd ed., 1933.

PORTER, A. K., *Lombard Architecture*, New Haven, 1915–17.

SALMI, M., *L'architettura romanica in Toscana*, Milan-Rome, 1927.

PUIG I CADAFALCH, J., *Le premier art roman*, Paris, 1928.

PUIG I CADAFALCH, J., *La géographie et les origines du premier art roman*, Paris, 1935.

FOCILLON, H., *Art d'Occident*, Paris, 1938.

GRODECKI, L., *L'architecture ottonienne*, Paris, 1958.

VAULTING PROBLEMS IN MEDIEVAL ARCHITECTURE

A general review in P. Frankl, *The Gothic*, Princeton, 1960.

ROMANESQUE ARCHITECTURE

BELGIUM–HOLLAND

VERMEULEN, F. A. J., *Handboek tot de Geschiedenis der Nederlandsche Bouwkunst*, The Hague, 1923 f.

BRIGODE, S., *Les églises romanes en Belgique*, 3rd ed., Brussels, 1944.

TER KUILE, E., *De Bouwkunst van de Middeleeuwen: De Architectuur* (Vol. I of *Duizend Jaar Bouwen in Nederland*), Amsterdam, 1948.

ENGLAND

CLAPHAM, A. W., *English Romanesque Architecture before the Conquest*, Oxford, 1930.

CLAPHAM, A. W., *English Romanesque Architecture after the Conquest*, Oxford, 1934.

RICE, D. TALBOT, *English Art*, 871–1100 (The Oxford History of English Art), Oxford, 1952.

SALZMAN, L. F., *Building in England down to 1540*, Oxford, 1952.

WEBB, G., *Architecture in Britain: The Middle Ages* (Pelican History of Art), Baltimore, 1956.

FRANCE–GENERAL

LASTEYRIE, R. DE, *L'architecture religieuse en France à l'époque romane*, Paris, 1912, 2nd ed., 1929. – Still a basic reference work.

BAUM, J., *Romanesque Architecture in France*, 2nd ed., London, 1928. – A book of standard pictures.

DESHOULIÈRES, F., *Au début de l'art roman: les églises de l'onzième siècle en France*, Paris, 1929, 2nd ed., 1943.

VALLERY-RADOT, J., *Églises romanes, filiations et échanges d'influences*, Paris, 1931.

DESHOULIÈRES, F., *Éléments datés de l'art roman en France*, Paris, 1936.

EVANS, J., *Art in Mediaeval France*, 987–1498, London, 1948.

NORMANDY

RUPRICH-ROBERT, V., *L'architecture normande aux XIe et XIIe siècles en Normandie et en Angleterre*, Paris, 1884–89. – Still a basic survey.

GALL, E., *Niederrheinische und normannische Architektur im Zeitalter der Frühgotik*, I., Berlin, 1915.

GALL, E., *Die Gotische Baukunst in Frankreich und Deutschland*. I., Leipzig, 1925. 2nd rev. ed., Brunswick, 1955. Both Gall studies are important to an understanding of Norman Romanesque architecture.

ANFRAY, M., *L'architecture normande. Son influence dans le Nord de la France aux XIe et XIIe siècles*, Paris, 1939.

BONY, J., "La technique normande du mur épais à l'époque romane," *Bulletin monumental*, XCVIII, 1939, pp. 153 ff.

BURGUNDY

DICKSON, M., and C., *Les églises romanes de l'ancien diocèse de Châlons, Cluny et sa région*, Mâcon, 1935.

VIREY, J., *Les églises romanes de l'ancien diocèse de Mâcon, Cluny et sa région*, Mâcon, 1935.

OURSEL, C., *L'art de Bourgogne*, Paris-Grenoble, 1953.

OURSEL, R., and A.-M., *Les églises romanes de l'Autunois et du Brionnais, Cluny et sa région*, Mâcon, 1956.

POITOU

CROZET, R., *L'art roman en Poitou*, Paris, 1948.

NIVERNAIS–LE PUY–LANGUEDOC

THIOLLIER, F., and N., *L'architecture religieuse à l'époque romane dans l'ancien diocèse du Puy*, Le Puy, 1900.

REY, R., *La sculpture romane languedocienne*, Toulouse, 1936.

ANFRAY, M., *L'architecture religieuse du Nivernais au moyen-âge. Les églises romanes*, Paris, 1951.

GERMANY

DEHIO, G., (E. GALL successor), *Handbuch der Deutschen Kunstdenkmäler*, Munich, 1906 f.

HAUPT, A., *Die älteste Kunst insbesondere die Baukunst der Germanen*, Berlin, 1909, 2nd ed., 1923. – Now almost wholly outdated.

FRANKL, P., *Die frühmittelalterliche und romanische Baukunst*, Potsdam, 1926. – Particularly important for Romanesque architecture in Germany.

DEHIO, G., *Geschichte der deutschen Kunst*, 4th ed., Berlin-Leipzig, 1930.

PINDER, W., *Die Kunst der deutschen Kaiserzeit bis zum Ende der staufischen Klassik*, Leipzig, 1935.

KUBACH, H. E., "Die vorromanische und romanische Baukunst in Mitteleuropa," *Zeitschrift für Kunstgeschichte*, XVIII, 1955, pp. 157–198. – Important survey of the recent literature.

GALL, E., *Dome und Klosterkirchen am Rhein*, Munich, 1956.

Neue Ausgrabungen in Deutschland, Berlin, 1958.

IRELAND

LEASK, H. G., *Irish Churches and Monastic Building*: I. *The First Phase and the Romanesque*, Chester Springs, Pa., 1955.

ITALY

DARTEIN, F. DE, *Étude sur l'architecture lombarde*, Paris, 1865 f.

BERTAUX, E., *L'art dans l'Italie méridionale*, Paris, 1904. – Still basic.

RIVOIRA, G. T., *Lombardic Architecture: its Origin, Development and Derivatives,* trans., by G. Mc. N. Rushforth, Oxford, 1910, 2nd ed., 1933.

PORTER, A. K., *Lombard Architecture,* New Haven, 1915–17. – Still unsurpassed as a *corpus* of the monuments.

RICCI, C., *Romanesque Architecture in Italy,* London, New York, 1925. – A book of standard pictures.

SALMI, M., *L'architettura romanica in Toscana,* Milan–Rome, 1927. – A useful compendium of the monuments.

KRAUTHEIMER, R., "Lombardische Hallenkirchen," *Jahrbuch für Kunstwissenschaft,* 1928, pp. 189 f.

KRAUTHEIMER, R., "San Nicola in Bari und die apulische Architektur des 12. Jahrhunderts," *Wiener Jahrbuch für Kunstgeschichte,* IX, 1934, pp. 5 f. – A single building studied against the broad background of northern and Italian Romanesque architecture.

VERZONE, P., *L'architettura romanica nel Vercellese,* Vercelli, 1934.

VERZONE, P., *L'architettura romanica nel Novarese,* Novara, 1935–36.

THÜMMLER, H., "Die Baukunst des 11. Jahrhunderts in Italien," *Römisches Jahrbuch für Kunstgeschichte,* III, 1939, pp. 183 f. – A comprehensive view of Italian Romanesque within the European framework.

ARATA, G., *Architettura medioevale in Sicilia,* Novara, 1942.

HORN, W., "Romanesque Churches in Florence and their Chronology and Stylistic Development," *Art Bulletin,* XXV, 1943, pp. 112 f.. – Interesting particularly for its methodology based on masonry and capital studies.

DELOGU, R., *L'architettura del medioevo in Sardegna,* Rome, 1953.

CERCHI, C., *Architettura romanica genovese,* Milan, 1954.

WILLEMSEN, C. A., and ODENTHAL, D., *Apulia, imperial splendor in southern Italy,* New York, 1959.

KRÖNIG, W., "Contributi all'Architettura Pugliese del Medioevo," *Atti del IX° Congresso Nazionale di Storia dell'Architettura, Bari, 1955,* Rome, 1959, pp. 39–66.

CREMA, L., "L'architettura medievale in Piemonte," *Atti del X° Congresso Nazionale di Storia dell'Architettura, Torino, 1957,* Rome, 1959, pp. 235–65.

SPAIN

LAMPÉREZ Y ROMEA, V., *Historia de la arquitectura cristiana española en la edad media,* Madrid, 1908–09.

PUIG I CADALFALCH, J., *et al., L'arquitectura romànica a Catalunya,* Barcelona, 1909–18. – A basic *corpus* of monuments.

GÓMEZ-MORENO, M., *Iglesias mozarabes,* Madrid, 1919.

FRISCHAUER, S., *Altspanischer Kirchenbau,* Berlin-Leipzig, 1930.

BEVAN, B., *History of Spanish Architecture,* London, 1938.

Ars Hispaniae, historia del arte hispánico (series in progress), Madrid, 1947 f.

SWITZERLAND

HECHT, J., *Der romanische Kirchenbau des Bodenseegebietes,* Basel, 1928.

REINHARDT, H., *Die kirchliche Baukunst in der Schweiz,* Basel, 1947. – A brief but authoritative survey.

LATE ROMANESQUE ARCHITECTURE

WEISE, G., *Die deutsche und die französische Kunst im Zeitalter der Staufer*, Mainz, 1948.

MEYER-BARKHAUSEN, W., *Das grosse Jahrhundert Kölnischer Kirchenbaukunst*, Cologne, 1952. — An intensive view of a major center of Late Romanesque architecture.

CISTERCIAN ARCHITECTURE

(not included for discussion in this volume)

AUBERT, M., *L'architecture cistercienne en France*, Paris, 1943.

DIMIER, M. A., *Recueil de plans d'églises cisterciennes*, Paris, 1949.

EYDOUX, H.-P., *L'architecture des églises cisterciennes d'Allemagne*, Paris, 1952.

KRÖNIG, W., "Zur Erforschung der Zisterzienser-Architektur," *Zeitschrift für Kunstgeschichte*, XVI, 1953, pp. 222 f.

HAHN, H., *Die frühe Kirchenbaukunst der Zisterzienser, Untersuchungen zur Baugeschichte vom Kloster Eberbach im Rheingau und ihren europäischen Analogien im 12. Jahrhundert*, Berlin, 1957.

BUCHER, F., *Notre-Dame de Bonmont und die ersten Zisterzienserabteien der Schweiz*, Bern, 1957.

AUBERT, M., "Existe-t-il une architecture cistercienne?", *Cahiers de civilisation mediévale*, I, 1958, pp. 153 f.

FRACCARO DE LONGHI, L., *L'architettura delle chiese cistercensi italiane con particolare riferimento ad un gruppo omogeneo dell'Italia settentrionale*, Milan, 1958.

altar (Lat.—*mensa* or *altare*)—the table for the Eucharistic sacrifice; originally separate from the martyrium (q.v.); often portable, later usually fixed in one place over (or containing) a relic or relics (q.v.); after about 700 a relic deposit was required for the consecration of an altar.

arcosolium—a burial niche covered by an arch set into the wall of a catacomb gallery or burial chamber.

basilica—a building consisting of three or more parallel aisles in which the central aisle is higher than the side aisles; usually illuminated by windows in the wall over the colonnades dividing the nave (q.v.) from the side aisles. The window zone is called the *clerestory*.

basilica ad corpus—a church built near or over the tomb of a martyr (q.v.).

bifora—window or gallery openings divided into two arches on a colonnette. Similarly *trifora*—openings divided into three arches.

brandeum (pl. *brandea*)—an object which has touched a relic (q.v.).

burial ad sanctum (pl. *ad sanctos*)—burial of the faithful near a sacred relic or relics.

cantharus (Gr.—*kantharos*)—fountain.

catacomb—subterranean cemetery consisting of a network of galleries and chambers.

columbarium (pl. *columbaria; columba* = dove)—Late Antique catacomb cemeteries containing many small wall niches for funerary urns, resembling pigeon coops.

confessio (Lat.—confession)—a room, usually part of a crypt complex, containing or adjoining a sacred relic or martyrium.

crypt (Lat.—*crypta*; pl. *cryptae* = covered or hidden, not necessarily subterranean. In medieval terminology, any vaulted room)—generally a wholly or partly underground room, usually containing a relic (or relics).
a) *annular (or ring) crypt*—a partly underground, covered or vaulted corridor, following the curve of an apse; in the apsidal axis a straight passage leads back to a room (*confessio*) containing or facing the relic(s).
b) *corridor crypt*—various types; some like rectangular ring crypts; others consisting of intersecting passages resembling catacomb galleries.
c) *hall crypt*—various types and sizes; sometimes under an apse, frequently extending under the transept and/or nave or a whole church; containing inner supports (piers or columns) and generally groin vaulted.
d) *ambulatory crypt*—a compound crypt with many possible variations; an annular corridor surrounding a *confessio* is frequently compounded with niches or apses and rear crypts (q.v.).
e) *rear crypt*—various types; commonly a hall crypt attached to the apse end of a church (cf. Essen), often an extension of an interior hall, annular or ambulatory crypt.

heroon (pl. *heroa*)—pagan monuments commemorating important persons, e.g., divinized emperors; frequently funerary structures and central in plan.

loculus (lit.—a small place)—a simple rectangular grave in the ground of a catacomb gallery or burial chamber.

martyr (Gr.–*witness*)–a witness to the truth of the Gospels usually in the blood.

    a) *ad martyrem*–applied to an altar, a grave or services near or next to the tomb of a martyr or a relic deposit. (Cf. also *basilica ad corpus.*)

martyrium–holy site, usually comprising an object (cf. relic) which bears witness to the truth of the Gospels.

nave–the main longitudinal room of a church, center aisle of a basilica.

patrocinium (pl. *patrocinia*)–the dedication of a church to a particular patron saint (effected by the deposit of a relic(s) of the saint in the church, usually in or under the (main) altar.

pignora (Lat.–a pawn)–used in the same sense as *brandeum* (q.v.).

propyleum (Gr.–*propyleon*)–a gateway building.

relic–sacred object or spot, e.g., the tomb of Christ, the Holy Cross, also all or parts of the bodies of sainted martyrs. (Cf. also *brandea* and *pignora.*)

sub divo (lit.–under God)–i.e., in the open air, not enclosed or covered.

sub lege (lit.–under the Law)–the period of the Old Testament, before the time of Christ.–Afterwards: *sub gratia.*

transepts

    a) *continuous transept*–a transverse room at right angles and equal in height to the nave.

    b) *tripartite transept*–the transept arms are divided from the nave by colonnades.

    c) *dwarf transept*–the transept arms are lower in height than the nave; the arches leading to the side arms are lower than the arches to the apse and nave.

INDEX

Numbers in regular roman type refer to text pages; *italic* figures refer to the plates.

124

SOURCES OF ILLUSTRATIONS

Alinari, Florence: 74, 75, 76, 93, 100

Anderson-Alinari: 65, 67, 72, 99

Archives Photographiques: 6, 38, 39, 47, 55, 57, 60, 61, 69, 70, 81, 82, 83, 89, 91, 96, 97

Dr. H. Beseler, Bonn: 32

H. Beseler, H. Roggenkamp, *Die Michaeliskirche in Hildesheim* (Berlin, 1954): 29, 31

Biblioteca del Gabinetto Disegni e Stampe degli Uffizi, Florence: 63

Bibliothèque Nationale, Paris: 17

W. Boeckelmann, "Grundformen im frühkarolingischen Kirchenbau des östlichen Frankenreiches," *Wallraf-Richartz Jahrbuch*, XVIII, 1956: 3

Brogi-Alinari, Florence: 71

J. Puig i Cadafalch, La Géographie et les Origines du Premier Art Roman (Paris, 1935): 37, 59

H. Claussen, "Spaetkarolingische Umgangskrypten im Saechsischen Gebiet," *Forschungen... III. Karolingische und Ottonische Kunst*, 1957: 35

K. J. Conant, *Carolingian and Romanesque Architecture:* (Baltimore, 1959): 11, 48

F. H. Crossley, Chester, England: 79

G. Forsyth, *The Church of St. Martin at Angers* (Princeton, 1953): 4, 21

P. Frankl, *Die frühmittelalterliche und romanische Baukunst* (Wildpark-Potsdam 1926): 88

S. Frischauer, *Altspanischer Kirchenbau* (Berlin-Leipzig, 1930): 6

L. Grodecki, *L'Architecture ottonienne* (Paris, 1958): 44

Institute of Fine Arts, New York: 22, 49

G. Kidder-Smith, New York: 68

E. Kluckhohn, "Gestalt und Geschichte der Ambrosiuskirche in Mailand," *Mitteilungen des kunsthistorischen Institutes in Florenz*, VI, 1940: 92

R. Krautheimer, "San Nicola in Bari und die apulische Architektur des 12. Jahrhunderts," *Wiener Jahrbuch für Kunstgeschichte*, IX, 1934: 66

R. de Lasteyrie, *L'Architecture Religieuse en France à l'Époque Romane* (Paris, 1929): 56, 85

Foto Marburg, Marburg/Lahn: 12, 24, 33, 34, 42, 43, 45, 46, 54, 84, 86, 87

Foto Mas, Barcelona: 5, 7, 58

Medieval Academy of America, Cambridge: 51, 52, 53 (courtesy K. J. Conant)

National Buildings Record, London: 2, 80

Dr. Franz L. Pelgen, Speyer/Rhein: 50

N. Pevsner, *Europäische Architektur* (Munich, 1957): 15

A. Kingsley Porter, *Lombard Architecture* (New Haven, 1915–17): 8

Howard Saalman: 18, 23, 40, 41

Helga Schmidt-Glassner, Stuttgart: 13, 19, 28, 94, 95

Schweiz. Landesmuseum, Zurich: 14

Soprintendenza ai Monumenti, Milan: 9

Soprintendenza ai Monumenti, Naples: 64

Stiftsbibliothek, St. Gallen: 20

Rev. F. Sumner, Durham: 78

H. Thümmler, "Die Baukunst des 11. Jahrhunderts in Italien," *Römisches Jahrbuch für Kunstgeschichte*, III, 1939: 73, 98

H. Thümmler, "Die karolingische Baukunst in Westfalen," *Forschungen... III, Karolingische und Ottonische Kunst*, 1957: 36

Roger Viollet, Paris: 10, 62, 90

G. Webb, *Architecture in Britain: The Middle Ages* (Baltimore, 1956): 77

Helmut Wegener, Hildesheim: 30

W. Zimmermann, *Das Münster zu Essen* (Essen, 1956): 25, 26, 27

Printed in photogravure and letterpress by Joh. Enschedé en Zonen, Haarlem, The Netherlands. Set in Romulus with Spectrum display, both faces designed by Jan van Krimpen. Format by William and Caroline Harris.